YOUR GUIDE TO

BETTER

PLANNING

*DISCOVER THE SECRETS TO BECOMING
MORE EFFECTIVE TOMORROW
THAN YOU ARE TODAY.*

Volume 3

OF

THE EFFECTIVENESS GUIDE

BY

EDWARD J. MURPHY

Never STOP Learning!

WHAT OTHER SAY ABOUT
The Effectiveness Institute

"I highly recommend the books from The Effectiveness Institute as texts for new leaders and a review for seasoned leaders - as a reminder of what they should be doing. These books are unique because they're replete with valuable information that you can actually learn today and use tomorrow. If you want to become absolutely essential to any organization, these books are for you."

- Dennis D. Cavin
Lieutenant General, US Army (Retired)
Vice President Army and Missile Defense Programs
Lockheed Martin, Corporate Business Development

"I recommend the books from The Effectiveness Institute because Ed Murphy doesn't theorize; he draws on his extensive experience from many years of service in the US Military and from working as an Executive Coach in Corporate America. His keen insights and practical advice make these books required reading for anyone trying to negotiate the maze of organizational chaos."

- Lee Lacy
Assistant Professor
US Army Warfighter Book
Command and General Staff College

"The books from The Effectiveness Institute will help you become more effective at work and in life. They will also help you unlock your potential and direct your team to greater success. I highly recommend these books."

- Lance Revo
Principal Engineering Design Specialist
Cyber Security at AREVA NP

I DEDICATE

THIS BOOK

TO

My Dear Friend and Partner,

JASON BOWNE

Jason, it's great having you as my partner and friend in this great work. You are a true friend. I'm thrilled to see all that you've accomplished in your lifetime. I know that you are destined for far greater things. I'm so proud of you. You showed me the secret to one of life's greatest paradoxes:

"WE ARE WHAT WE LEAVE BEHIND.'

You and Michelle have raised such a great family."

Other Books From
THE EFFECTIVENESS INSTITUTE

Here are the eleven volumes from *The Effectiveness Institute*, one for each Core Competencies of Effectiveness:

VOLUME 1: The Power of FOLLOWERSHIP

VOLUME 2: The Power of DELEGATING

VOLUME 3: The Power of PLANNING

VOLUME 4: The Power of ORGANIZING

VOLUME 5: The Power of COMMUNICATING

VOLUME 6: The Power of PROBLEM-SOLVING

VOLUME 7: The Power of AWARENESS

VOLUME 8: The Power of TRAINING

VOLUME 9: The Power of MOTIVATION

VOLUME 10: The Power of CHARACTER

All the above books are available at *Amazon.com*

Never STOP Learning!

This page is intentionally left blank.

CONTENTS

PREFACE

I'm often asked, "What does the picture mean on the cover of your book?"

This picture is a metaphor for the dilemma young people face when coming from school to the world-of-work.

They're unprepared, do not have the right tools, the right motivation, nor any clue of what's most important to every employer on the planet.

The cover image shows a young man rowing a boat in the fog. If you look closer, you'll notice that the boat is too small for the person in it. You can tell because one side of the boat is dipping so low in the water that it's almost taking on water. You can also tell that he has little experience in a boat because the other side of the boat is way out of the water because his weight is not evenly distributed.

He is also rowing in dense fog. He cannot see where he's going. The further he gets from shore; he cannot turn around and head back because he has no idea from which direction he came.

Finally, since he's not wearing a flotation device, he's assuming he won't have to swim. You know where assumptions take you, right? He is totally unprepared.

He didn't plan his trip, nor is he prepared to deal with the consequences of what lies ahead. He is, or will soon be, lost and at the mercy of nature.

Such is the fate of young workers today.

In today's job market, there's a huge skills gap between graduation and the first day on the job. As a result, young people lack the job skills needed to "hit-the-ground-running" and find themselves in dead-end, menial, minimum-wage jobs, trading time for money just to put food on the table. And it will take them decades before they're effective enough to *add value* to any employer. What a waste!

How do I know that? I know it because I've spent 20+ years of my life as an executive coach, working with hundreds of business executives and small business owners, seeking the answer to this simple question:

Why are some people more effective than others?

What do they think, say, and do that made them more effective?

During that time, I was privileged to work with some of the most exceptional men and women in America. Through their example, I learned the true definition of effectiveness by documenting what they did, how they did it, and most importantly, how they made people feel. What you'll find here is the result of my years of research.

Today, my purpose in life is to help you navigate the world-of-work, maximize your true career potential, and become more effective and successful at work and in life.

ENJOY!

INTRODUCTION

*"Planning is bringing the future into the present so
that you can do something about it now."*
- Alan Lakein

This book is about *PLANNING!*

**Planning is your ability to create Plans of Action
that bridge the gap from where you are to where you want
to be and Contingency Plans for when things go wrong.**

Planning is also one of these eleven Core Competencies of your
effectiveness and success at work and in life.

*Followership, Delegating, Planning, Organizing, Communicating,
Problem-Solving, Decision-Making, Awareness, Training,
Motivating and Character.*

This book is for everyone in the workforce who reports to another person
for their work assignments, including employees working for an employer
and small business owners, entrepreneurs, and the self-employed working
for customers, clients, or patients.

*Simply stated, this book is for you regardless of
your occupation, position, or level of authority.*

You may not realize that *Planning* is one the most powerful and underrated
transferrable skills in business today.

If you're unable to demonstrate your ability to create plans to resolve
problems, achieve goals, or conduct activities, well, you can guess the
consequences.

This happens because many people in the workforce are afraid to accept
greater responsibility for fear of failure.

They also lack an understanding of how to use the right tools and
techniques, collaborate and build consensus with a team, conduct a risk
assessment, mitigate risk, anticipate unintended consequences and 2d and
3d order effects, create contingency and mitigation plans, eliminate
unresolved issues, conduct a Backbriefing, and manage a budget – all of
which are addressed in this book.

Without these abilities, you'll be wasting your career sitting on the
sidelines, watching others move ahead while wondering why?

I speak from 24 years as a US Army Officer and 20 years as an Executive Coach in Corporate America in Seattle, San Diego, Kansas City, and Phoenix.

As an Executive Coach, I was blessed to work with some of America's most successful men and women, including hundreds of business executives, teams, and small business owners.

I documented what they said, did, how they did it, what worked and what didn't. But, most importantly, I documented how they made people feel.

As a result, I learned that the most effective and successful people stood out because they were able to do these two things better than anyone else:

- First, to consistently produce excellent results.

- Second, to add value to those who helped produce those results.

This book will enhance your ability to do both.

The fact is that you may be the top producer, but if you haven't added value to those who helped you, especially your boss, you'll never become effective or successful, period.

What new skills or abilities have you acquired in the last twelve months? What contributions have you made to your current position since this time last year?

And, most of all, what are you doing about it?

This book is unique because it:

- Gives you the most actionable tactics, techniques, and tools needed to consistently produce excellent results.

- Teaches you the best practices used every day by the most effective and successful people in their field, which you were never taught in school.

- Provides you with step-by-step instructions explaining what and how things should be done that you won't find anywhere in academia or Corporate America to help you maximize your true potential.

- Contains everything you want to know about *Planning*, plus everything you didn't realize you need to know about how *Planning* enhances your effectiveness and success in business.

I know that by learning, using, and sharing the best practices found here, you'll be well on your way to becoming more effective and successful.

Remember, no matter how good you think you are; you can always be better.

So, what are you waiting for? You have too much to lose by not taking a more active role in your Professional Development.

When you're ready to *elevate-your-game* to the next level, join us on this incredible *Journey of Discovery*.

Also, if you feel this information could help someone else, please let them know. If it turns out to make a difference in their life, they'll be forever grateful to you, as will I.

Never STOP Learning!

Ed

Founder of *The Effectiveness Institute*
email: ed.murphy77@gmail.com

Stop wishing you were better and do something about it today!

This page is intentionally left blank.

1
THE POWER OF PLANNING

"It takes as much energy to wish as it does to plan."
- Eleanor Roosevelt

This book will give you a far better understanding of *Planning*, its importance, and how to do it better than anyone else.

Planning is your ability to create Plans of Action that bridge the gap from where you are to where you want to be and Contingency Plans for when things go wrong.

Planning provides direction, reduces risk, reduces overlapping and wasteful activities, promotes innovation and creativity, sets objectives, and develops courses of action for better decision-making.

Here, you'll learn to use the most actionable *tactics, techniques, and tools* needed to master the *Art of Planning*. As an executive coach for over 20 years, I know what your boss and customers expect, especially regarding your effectiveness and success at work. The only important question is,

Effective people know that their ability to plan is critical to their effectiveness and success at work. By learning, using, and sharing these *best practices*, you'll be well on your way to becoming the one person who adds the greatest value to the team - making you essential.

Also, to make this book easier to understand, I'll be using the term "boss" instead of leader, employer, or customer. I do this because if you're an employee, your boss is your employer. And if you're self-employed or a small business owner, your boss is your customer, client, or patient.

This means that you'll always be working for a boss - whoever pays you for your products or services.

This also means that you'll always be a *follower of someone - whoever pays you for your work.

*To learn more about **Followership**, available at **Amazon.com,** see page 5.

So, let's get to work!

What do bosses need most to survive?

Every boss needs effective followers who can resolve problems and achieve goals. And any effective follower knows how to turn any assignment (a problem, goal, event, or activity) into a simple project and manage it to successful completion.

Step 5. Create your Risk Matrix.

Here's an example of a Risk Matrix.

Risk Matrix for Team Building Session			
BAD SITUATION	**IMPACT**	**PROBABILITY**	**CONPLAN**
Guests Arriving Late	Significant (8-10)	Medium (4-7)	A
Transport to Resort	Moderate (4-7)	Medium (4-7)	B
Lost Baggage	Minor (1-3)	High (8-10)	C

Notice that this simple table shows all Bad Internal Situations, their Impact, Probability, and which CONPLAN to use. The risk numbers 1 - 10 are used to help create your Risk Threshold.

Step 7. Staff your CONPLANs.

Staff your CONPLANs through all Key Players for their concurrence or non-concurrence with comments (Chapter 16).

As far as your boss is concerned, your effectiveness or value-added is a function of your ability to successfully manage projects. And you don't need to be a *certified project manager* to manage projects successfully. All you need is a basic understanding of a few tactics, techniques, and tools, which you'll learn here.

The better you get at managing projects, the more value you bring to your boss. And for every project, you'll encounter obstacles along the way. All you need to do is to convert each obstacle into another project and make it go away.

What's a Project?

I define a project as an assignment that requires the effort of others. Anything you can do yourself is a task and not a project. So, whenever you get stuck at work, just realize there's a simple way to re-frame anything into a project to get things moving again.

What's a Plan of Action?

Every project needs a good *Plan of Action*, even if it's only a mental plan or a sketch on the back of a napkin. Any good *Plan of Action (POA)* format (Appendix A) has at least six components:

- **Objective:** Who, What, Where, When, and Why (Appendix A)?

- **Methods:** How will we accomplish this Objective (Appendix A)?

- **Timetable:** Planning backward from today, how can we use the time available to plan and prepare (Appendix A and Chapter 2)?

- **Resources:** What will you need (Appendix A)?

- **Unresolved Issues:** What are all the things (questions, unknowns, concerns, shortfalls, obstacles, or problems) that could slow or stop your progress (Appendix A, Chapter 9)?

- **Risk:** What could *reasonably-go-wrong* and how can they be *mitigated* (Appendix A and Chapters 17-19)?

If you don't know a specific piece of information, still list the category, but show a TBD (To Be Determined). For example, if you don't know the end time of an activity, show, End time: TBD.

What's a Project's Life Cycle?

Every project has at least four phases: Planning, Preparing (before), Executing (during), and Assessing (After). For example, here's a *Gannt Chart* showing the four phases of a one-day project that begins in 30-days:

Typical Gannt Chart for a Project Starting in 30-Days.			
Phase 1	15	25	30
1	Planning IPR		
2		Preparing IPR	
3			Executing AAR
4	Assessing		

Notice that the *Assessing Phase* is conducted continuously throughout the project and is formalized using two *In-Progress Reviews* (or IPRs) (Chap 22), numerous *Project Updates* (not shown) (Chap 13), and one *After-Action Review* (or AAR) (Chap 34).

2
BY ASKING THE
RIGHT QUESTIONS

"The art and science of asking questions is the source of all knowledge."
- Thomas Berger

OBJECTIVE (Who, What, When, Where, and Why?)

- What's my access to sources of info, and who's this project for?
- Where and why is this project being conducted?
- How important is this project, and to whom is it important?
- How will success be measured, and who will measure it?
- What's the requirement, scope, and complexity of work?
- What's the limit of my authority (to decide, delegate, spend $, hire, and fire)?
- Does someone with authority approve this?
- When does this project start and end?
- What's the most important task for this project to be a success?
- Who has done this task before, and what were their problems, consequences, and effects?
- What must be ordered or started now?

METHODS (How)

- How should we do it? What are all our options, which is best?
- What needs to happen during the four phases of this project?
- What're all the tasks involved, and who are responsible for performing each task (called Key Players)?
- What must be done before, during, and after the project?
- What specific instructions do we have for those delegated a task?
- How many are expected to attend or are affected by this?
- What're our restrictions (can't do) and imperatives (must do)?
- Who has done this or a similar type of project before?
- How will this project be advertised or promoted?
- What are my responsibilities, expectations, duties, constraints, authority, and standards?
- Who're the most important people to talk to right now?
- What're the consequences if this turns out unsuccessful?

TIMETABLE (Chapter 7)

- Planning backward from today, when are the Planning, Preparing, Executing, and Assessment Phases?
- When's the *Backbriefing* (Chapter 12)?
- What's the *Project Update Briefing* schedule (Chapter 23)?
- Which *Preventive Actions* must be done during each phase (Chapter 6)?
- How long will each task take, and what's the best sequence of these tasks and *Preventive Actions?*
- Which tasks can't start or finish without another task starting or ending? (Dependent tasks)
- Which task needs to be started right now?
- What's the detailed schedule, program, and calendar?
- When's the rehearsal, and what will be rehearsed (Chapter 25)?
- What else is going on in the company or *community at the same time? What happened last year at this time?

*Do you really want your project to go on at the same time as Spring Break, the Superbowl, or a Presidential Election Voting Day?

RESOURCES

- What resources are most important for the success of this project?
- How much of each resource is needed, when, and where?
- Who's responsible (Key Player) for providing these resources?
- When's the latest time we need these resources delivered?
- Who's paying for this, and what must be ordered now?
- What skills, attitudes, or knowledge are needed, and who has the skills we need?
- Any special needs for safety, security, sanitation, disabilities?
- What're our *Shortfalls* (anything you need to complete a project that you don't have)?
- How much money can we spend? What's our Budget?

UNRESOLVED ISSUES (Chapter 9)

- What do we need to know but don't?

- What do we know for sure, but the answer is unsatisfactory or unacceptable?

- What are our shortfalls, which are things we need but don't have?

- What are all the questions, unknowns, concerns, shortfalls, obstacles, or problems that could slow or stop your progress?

- Who has done this type of work before, and what were their problems, consequences, and effects?

- What are we forgetting to do?

RISK (Chapters 17-19)

- **Physical: (Injury, Illness, or Death)**

  - ✓ Have we inspected the site for anything that could cause injury, illness, accident, or death?

  - ✓ Have we inspected for sanitation and access for those with disabilities?

- **Security: (Cyber and Physical)**

  - ✓ For Cybersecurity: What could cause a data breach, loss of personal info or intellectual property, or a disruption of services?

  - ✓ For Physical Security: What could cause unauthorized access leading to theft, fraud, waste, abuse, or property damage?

- **Financial:**

  - ✓ What could cause financial loss or property damage?

  - ✓ What insurance do we need, and is it *in-force*?

- **Operational:**

  See Chapter 18: Risk Assessment

This page is intentionally left blank.

3
BY KNOWING THE
PROBLEMS YOU'LL FACE

*"Great leaders are almost always great simplifiers, who can
cut through argument, debate, and doubt, to offer
a solution everybody can understand."*
- Colin Powell

Effective people know that their ability to resolve problems and make better *decisions is critical to their success. *Problem-Solving* is about making choices that range from the mundane to the life-changing.

Here are the most common types of business problems:

Level 1 Problems: "What Should I Do?"

These problems are really "Where can I find help to resolve this problem?" All human problems have an entire career field dedicated to their solution. If you have a legal problem, you ask a legal problem solver: an attorney. If you have a marital relationship problem, you might go to a marital counselor or an attorney. And for almost any problem, you can start your research on the web.

Level 2 Problems: "How Much?" or "How Many?"

These problems ask how much time, money, or other resources, are you willing to expend to resolve this problem. The answers here could range from everything (if you can afford it) to nothing (if you do it yourself) or somewhere in between. The only important issue is to allocate sufficient resources to ensure the real cause of the problem goes away.

Level 3 Problems: "Solution A" or "Solution B?"

Level 3 problems apply to problems like, "Should I do this myself or hire an expert?" which requires a simple "Me" or "Them." Your challenge now becomes deciding the better of the two by assessing their advantages and disadvantages. This normally involves questions like how much it will cost, how difficult will it be, and how long will it take?

*To learn more about **Decision-Making**, available at **Amazon.com,** see page 5.

Here's an example of a simple decision matrix.

Choice Between the Two		
Criteria	Solution A	Solution B
Total Cost	$100	$80
Degree Difficulty	Difficult	Moderate
Time to resolve	One Week	Three Weeks
Advantages	Shortest Time	Lowest Cost Least Difficult
Disadvantages	Highest Cost Most Difficult	Longest Time
Decision	?	?

This table displays the raw data for *total cost*, *degree of difficulty*, and the *time to resolve* the problem. Also, note the advantages and disadvantages of each solution - but the final decision rests with you.

Level 4 Problems: "Which Option is the BEST?"

Level 4 problems ask which option is BEST when you have three or more valid options. As such, this will require the use of a *Problem-Solving Process (or PSP)*. The PSP consists of these steps, where Decision-Making is just one step in that process:

Step 1: Define the Problem.
Step 2: Gather Facts and Assumptions.
Step 3: List Possible Options.
Step 4: Test Possible Options.
Step 5: Select the BEST Option.
Step 6: Create a Plan of Action (Appendix A).
Step 7: Execute the Plan of Action.
Step 8: Assess Progress and Results.

Level 5 Problems: Should I wait or just do nothing?

These problems are the ones that fall into the "grey area." These are problems that are sometimes better left alone, for various reasons, or they require you to wait before solving. When faced with a problem, can't you do nothing? Sure. Think about it. You have this option every time you're faced with a problem (Chapter 32). To learn more about keeping track of all your assignments (accepted and made) and changes, see Appendix E.

4
BY USING THE RIGHT TOOLS

"Never look back unless you are planning to go that way."
- Henry David Thoreau

The *Problem-Solving Process* is designed for problems that have more than two valid options. How can you ensure you select the Best person, product, company, or solution, especially if there are many options from which to choose? Use the *Problem-Solving Process* from this book and help keep your emotions (fear and pride) from getting in your way. Assuming that the problem statement has already been created, what tools can help you make the best decisions?

By using a Network Diagram

A Network Diagram maps out the structure of a network with various symbols and line connections.

A Network Diagram is a visual representation of a network's architecture.

It's ideal for sharing the layout of a network because the visual presentation makes it easier for users to understand how items are connected. Here's an example of a *Network Diagram*.

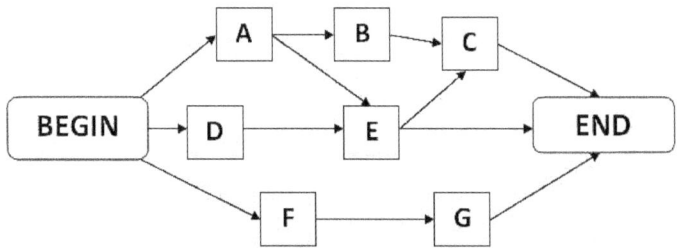

From this *Network Diagram*, notice that there are seven tasks (A-G). With your team, estimate how long each task will take. Example: Task D (one week). The critical path is the path that takes the longest time (example: From BEGIN to D to E to END). Once your Network Diagram is completed, it's time to create your Gantt Chart.

A Gantt chart is a bar chart that illustrates a project schedule.

Gantt charts illustrate the start and finish dates of the terminal elements and summary elements of a project. Terminal elements and summary elements constitute the work breakdown structure of the project. They also show the dependency (dependent and independent tasks) relationships between activities. Here's an example of a Gantt Chart (below) for an eleven-month project. Assume that today's date is 14 June, 20XX (see the vertical black line).

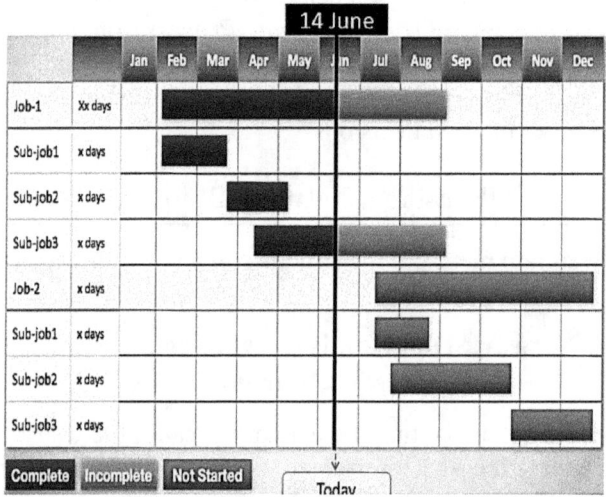

Notice that this chart shows a project with two jobs, each with three sub-jobs, on the left vertical axis and the months on the bottom horizontal axis. Each job/sub-job is represented with a horizontal line depicting the start and end dates. The width of each horizontal bar shows the duration time for each.

The color coding for each job/sub-job shows the current status for each using this color code:

- GREEN, which means *completed.*
- YELLOW, which means *incomplete.*
- RED, which means *not yet started.*

For example, it shows that Job 1 is almost two-thirds complete, and Job 2 will start in mid-July.

Gannt Charts monitor the progress of all jobs or tasks over time to determine if your project is on schedule with your plan. They help you determine, based on today's date, if the jobs or tasks that were <u>scheduled</u> to be completed have been completed? If not, why and what's being done to stay on schedule?

By using a Flowchart

A flowchart is a diagram that represents a workflow or process and is used in designing and documenting simple processes or programs.

The flowchart shows the steps as boxes of various kinds and their order by connecting them with arrows. Flowcharts are used in analyzing, designing, documenting, and managing a process or program.

Like other diagrams, they help you visualize what is going on and thereby help you understand a process and find less-obvious features, like flaws and bottlenecks.

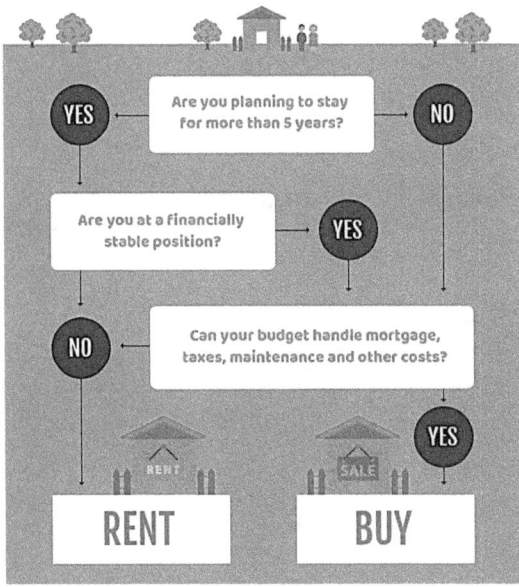

The two most common types of boxes in a flowchart are a processing step (usually called activity and denoted as a rectangular box) and a decision, which is usually represented as a diamond.

Flowcharts are the seven basic tools used for quality control, including histograms, Pareto charts, check sheets, control charts, cause-and-effect diagrams, and scatter diagrams.

Here are the four general types of flowcharts:

- Document flowcharts show how a document flows through a system.

- Data flowcharts show how data flows through a system.

- System flowcharts show controls at a physical or resource level.

- Program flowchart show the controls in a program within a system.

Notice that every type of flowchart focuses on control rather than on the particular flow itself. Generally, flowcharts flow from top to bottom or from left to right. Here are the basic shapes used:

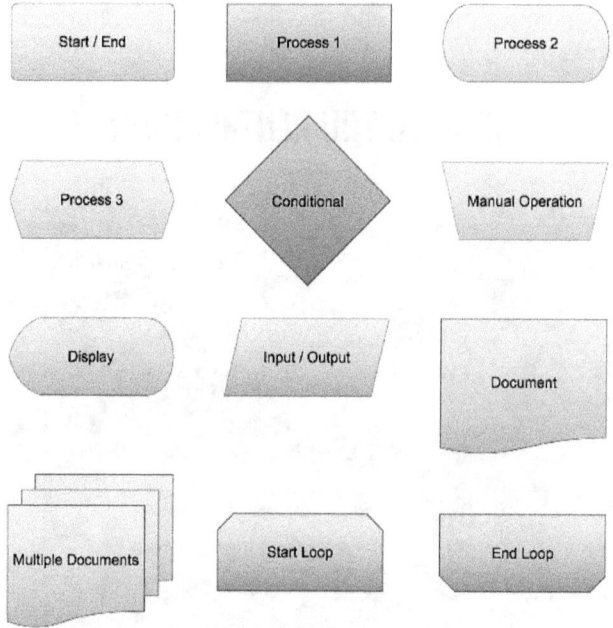

By using a Decision Tree

A decision tree is a decision support tool that uses a tree-like model, diagram, or chart of decisions and their possible consequences, including outcomes, costs, and utility.

People use decision trees to:

- Determine the Best Option or Course of Action.

- Show a statistical probability.

- Depict a decision and every potential outcome of making that decision.

Each branch of the decision tree represents a possible decision, outcome, or reaction. The farthest branches on the tree represent the results. By displaying a sequence of steps, a decision tree gives you an effective way to visualize and understand the potential options and their range of possible outcomes.

This structure allows you to take a problem with multiple possible solutions and display those solutions in a simple format that also shows the relationship between different events or decisions. Each end-result has an assigned risk and reward weight or number.

Here are the steps to create a Decision Tree:

Step 1: To make a decision tree, start by drawing a square at the top of a page. In that square, write the specific decision that needs to be made.

Step 2: Then, draw lines downward (or to the right) for each option. At the end of each line or option, analyze the results.

- If the result of an option is a new decision, draw a box at the end of that line, draw new lines out of that decision, representing the new options, and label them accordingly.

- If the result of an option is unclear, draw a circle at the end of the line, which denotes a potential risk.

- If an option results in a decision, leave that line blank.

Step 3: Continue to expand until every line reaches an endpoint, meaning you've covered every choice or outcome. Use a triangle to indicate the endpoint.

Here's an example of a decision tree.

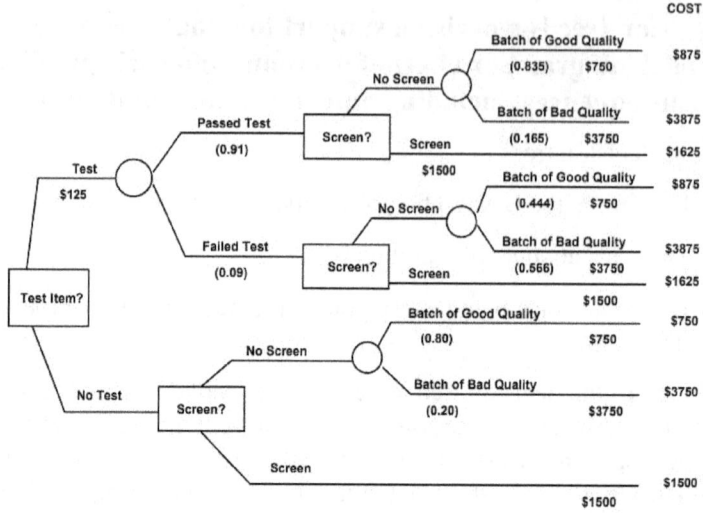

Here are the three most important components of a decision tree:

Root Node: This top-level node represents the ultimate objective or big decision you're trying to make.

Branches: Branches, which stem from the root, represent different options or courses of action. They are indicated with an arrow line and often include associated costs, as well as their probability.

Leaf Node: The leaf nodes attached at the end of the branches represent possible outcomes for each action.

There are two types of leaf nodes:

Square leaf nodes, which indicate another decision needs to be made

Circle leaf nodes, which indicate a chance event or unknown outcome.

Decision trees clarify choices, risks, objectives, and gains. The big advantage of decision trees is their predictive framework, which helps you map different possibilities and ultimately determine which option or course of action has the highest probability of success. This helps to safeguard your decisions against unnecessary risks or unintended consequences.

What's the difference between a flow chart and a decision tree?

Many people think that flow charts and decision trees are the same. Both tools offer a visual means of imparting information, but a decision tree has probabilities and costs or benefits. A flow chart doesn't. Flow charts and decision trees are very different tools.

- **A Flow Chart** shows the process flow (or steps), including what needs to be done and the proper sequence of activities required to resolve a problem, which may or may not involve a decision. It's typically used to display a process or for writing a computer program.

- **A Decision Tree** is a decision support tool that uses a tree-like model of decisions and their possible consequences, including chance event outcomes, resource costs, and utility. It shows the costs/benefits, conditional and joint probabilities of events occurring based on a stream of decision choices made. With a decision tree, the flow of activities isn't considered. Only decision-making points and their outcomes are considered.

By using Regression Analysis

The most common form of regression analysis, linear regression, is to find the line, as shown below, that most closely fits the data according to a specific mathematical criterion.

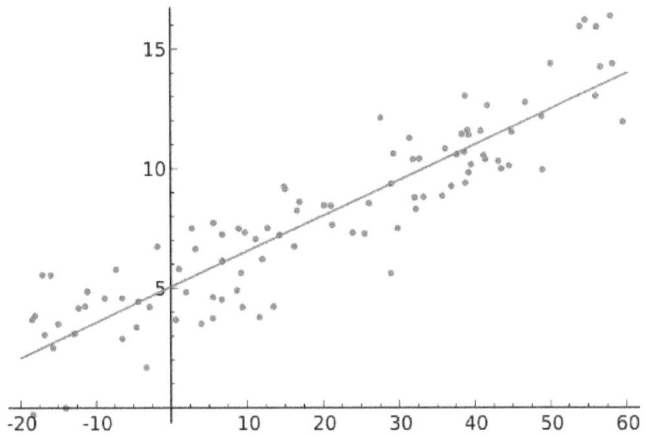

Regression Analysis helps predict, forecasting, and infer relationships between the independent and dependent variables.

A "degree of confidence" of 95% means that you have 95% confidence that the true score should be in the confidence interval.

"Degree of confidence" represents the probability that the confidence interval captures the true population parameter.

If you want 95% confidence that you're capturing the true population parameters, you may sometimes have to report a really wide interval. With a degree of confidence of 95%, you have 95% confidence that the true population parameters will be in the confidence interval. 95% is the standard.

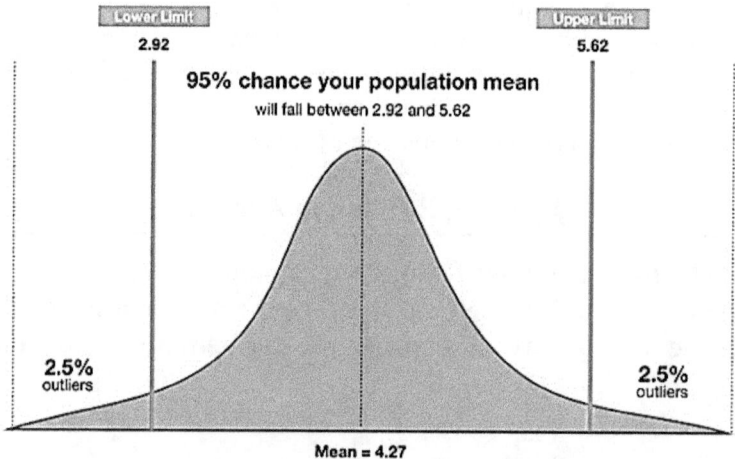

The definition of a "confidence interval" says that under repeated experiments, 95% of the time, this confidence interval will contain the true statistic.

To learn more about these tools, visit *KahnAcademy.org.*

5
BY USING THE
RIGHT TECHNIQUES

*"Sometimes you make the right decision, sometimes
you make the decision right."*
- Phil McGraw

In the workforce, there are countless decisions waiting for you to make. On the other hand, if you're starting, your decision may come in the form of a recommendation. Either way, both require you to make a decision.

By using Decision Points

Decision Points can be used in a variety of ways.

A Decision Point is a condition that, once met, triggers an action to be taken.

Here are a few examples of how they're used.

By eliminating accounts of little value

Let's assume you are responsible for ten major accounts. How low in "Annual Sales" would an account have to be before deciding to take some form of action? When is it no longer cost-effective to continue doing business with accounts that add little to your bottom-line?

In this example, once "Annual Sales" drop below a certain threshold, what action should be taken? What options exist from which to make a choice? Identify the criterion well in advance by carefully considering all the options (actions) you have available (like who does what, when?).

Carrying this example further, let's assume you have the following options (actions) available for any accounts whose "Annual Sales" numbers drop below (condition) the previous year.

Here's an example of a simple Account Assessment Matrix.

Condition: If Annual Sales Drop Below Previous Year		
BY:	ACTION	CONPLAN
0 – 5.9 %	Contact client directly	A
6 – 9.9 %	Set up meeting with client and boss	B
10+ %	Set up meeting with client and our CEO	C

For example, in January, if Company A's annual sales are 7.2 % below the previous year's sales: CONPLAN B would be executed requiring that a meeting be scheduled between your boss and the senior management of Company A to see what is causing the decrease and to determine what can be done to increase sales. There are many options (actions) you could create. However, the question remains, what must happen (conditions) before any action is initiated? Ensure this document is *Staffed* (Chapter 16) through all *Key Players* and approved by the Decision Maker.

By avoiding cost overruns

Another way to use decision points is to avoid cost overruns. Let's assume that your boss is concerned that the budget estimate for your project is too low. He thinks it will cost much more, and he wants to know what cost controls can be put in place to stop the project if costs get too expensive.

Here's an example of a simple Budget Control Matrix.

Trident Project Budget: $200,000		
Over by:	Action	CONPLAN
25 %	Initiate cost controls - no major expenditures	A
50%	Impose cost controls. No discretionary spending	B
100%	Terminate Project ASAP	C

- If the cost exceeds **25%, CONPLAN A** will be activated that stops any further expenditures on

- If the cost exceeds **50 %, CONPLAN B** is activated that stops all discretionary expenditures.

- If the cost exceeds **100%, CONPLAN C** is activated that terminates the project.

By using a Decision Support Template

A Decision Support Template (DST) is a table created in advance to help you decide to act (take a particular course of action) more quickly once the decision criterion is known.

DSTs are used when response time is at a minimum, like when making crisis decisions by *Emergency Response Teams*. Most decisions in life aren't normally made this way because time is usually not a concern. Occasionally, you need a system to help you decide quickly to either open doors A, B, or C based on the conditions at that time, especially if you know that you'll have little time to think about it when it comes time to decide. Think about the decision in advance and prepare a DST. DST's typically support and are an appendix to a *Contingency Plan*.

For example, let's say you need to decide where the company picnic will be held (either outdoors or indoors). The obvious determining factor is the weather. By talking with last year's Project Leader, everyone was soaking wet from the rain. Being a student of *Murphy's Law*, you decide to reserve both a local park (if good weather) and a local high school gymnasium (if bad weather).

But here's the dilemma. You need to make a weather decision because you'll need at least two hours of setup time for all the food, beverages, and entertainment. You decide to make a final weather decision two hours before the picnic starts so members will know where to go to set up.

How are you going to figure out what the weather's going to do? You could use the local weather report. But how accurate are weather reports? You decide to use two different criteria: The local weather report and s spotter on the ground at the picnic site.

Here's an example of a *Decision Support Template*:

		Weather from Spotter at Park	
		RAIN	NO RAIN
Local Weather Report	RAIN	Gym	Local Park (**Risk**)
	NO RAIN	Gym	Local Park

Question: Two hours before the company picnic, is it the Local Park (outside) or the Gymnasium (inside)? Using this DST, only one option (upper right, above) is at <u>Risk</u>. How could you mitigate this risk? You could find and reserve a park that has a pavilion or other overhead cover.

Ensure this document is *Staffed* (Chapter 16) through all *Key Players, approved by your boss,* and rehearse a few days before your project starts. Now, you've beaten *Murphy's Law*. Nice work! Let it pour!

How else can Decision Support Templates be used?

Here's another example of how to use a Decision-Support Template.

		Probability		
		Low	Medium	High
Impact	Minor	1	2	3
	Moderate	4	5	6
	Significant	7	8	9

Notice that this template has two tables and can measure risk based on its probability and impact.

#	Actions Required	CONPLAN
1	No action needed. Monitor for changes.	
2	Medium - Minor	A
3	High - Minor	B

Based on your Probability and Impact assessment, this matrix gives you a way to explain what actions should be taken and which CONPLAN should be used (Chapter 17). And here's an example of a National DST created by the CDC during the Covid 19 Pandemic.

Unvaccinated People	Your Activity	Fully Vaccinated People
	Outdoor	
	Walk, run, or bike outdoors with members of your household	
	Attend a small, outdoor gathering with fully vaccinated family and friends	
	Attend a small, outdoor gathering with fully vaccinated and unvaccinated people	
	Dine at an outdoor restaurant with friends from multiple households	
	Attend a crowded, outdoor event, like a live performance, parade, or sports event	

By using an Authorization Matrix

Effective people know that decision-making authority should be *delegated down to the lowest level possible.

An Authorization Matrix is a table created to enable your team members to make decisions in designated situations without direct supervision.

Have you ever been in any of these situations at work?

- When a simple decision needed to be made to move the work forward, your boss was unavailable.

- When you were told that no one could make a simple decision because they were waiting for you.

- When you found out that one of your team members made a decision yesterday that you felt was a mistake.

If you had an *Authorization Matrix*, you wouldn't have to worry about either of these. Your members need to know who's authorized to make which kinds of decisions. This is where an authorization matrix can help you.

*To learn more about **Delegating**, available at **Amazon.com,** see page 5.

Here are the most important steps.

Step 1. List all possible situations that require a decision.

With the help of your team, list all the possible situations that could occur that require a decision. Knowing that some decisions need to be made at the lowest possible level, decide which decisions you'll keep for yourself only.

Step 2. Create an Authorization Matrix.

Create an *Authorization Matrix* showing what decisions need to be made and who is authorized to make them. Drive decision-making authority down to the lowest level.

Step 3. Train your team members.

Train your team on how to make good decisions. Groom them for success.

Here's an example of an *Authorization Matrix*:

Authorization Matrix			
Who can make this decision?	Team Leader	A-Team Leader	Team Member
To spend over $1,000	X		
To spend less than $1,000		X	
To change a requirement	X		
To change a process		X	
To cancel...			X
To Stop or Reject...			X

Step 4. Post the matrix.

Post this matrix for all team members to see and use.

Step 5. Hold them accountable.

Hold them accountable for their decisions and the results and give all the credit to them when the results are good.

Intuition is your ability to acquire knowledge without proof, evidence, or conscious reasoning or without understanding how the knowledge was acquired, including unconscious cognition, inner sensing, and inner insight to unconscious pattern-recognition. Thus, intuition is a powerful unseen force, especially in decision-making.

Intuition is the process of receiving input and ideas without knowing how or from where it came.

Intuitive decision-making is far more than common sense because it involves additional sensors to perceive and gain awareness of what is going on within and around you. It's also known as an inner sense, inner voice, a prompting, or a spiritual guide. Intuition comes from a higher consciousness and enters your *awareness into your core (your Spirit) and is active when you clearly know something is true, but you can't explain how or why you know it. As you listen to your Spirit within, that still small voice will whisper to you and prompt you to act. Or it may come in the form of someone who mysteriously appears in your life – just in the *nick-of-time*.

In *The Soul of Leadership*, **Dr. Deepak Chopra** calls intuition *The Secret of Synchronicity.*

He defines synchronicity as more than a meaningful coincidence, altering events to bring in more meaning.

An example might be when you meet someone unexpectedly that has the exact answer to a problem you've been facing.

What abilities are essential to effective decision-making?

The three most powerful abilities you have that are essential to effective decision-making and your survival are:

Intellect comes from your rational mind and is active when you use your brain to learn and process information.

Instinct comes from within your body and communicates positive and negative reactions, like the fight or flight response when you feel fear.

Intuition comes from a higher consciousness and enters your awareness into your core (your Spirit) and is active when you clearly know the truth, but you can't explain it (like when you know something about a person before they tell you).

*To learn more about *Awareness*, available at **Amazon.com,** see page 5.

How can intuition help you make better decisions?

Here's an incredible true story to illustrate the Power of Intuition.

> *"One day, a fire company responded to what they thought was a typical kitchen fire. As the Fire Chief observed his Firefighter battling the fire, he noticed that the heat was much greater than a normal kitchen fire, and the blaze couldn't be extinguished – regardless of how much water was used. The Chief sensed something was wrong and immediately ordered the evacuation of the building. Minutes later, the kitchen floor collapsed because the main fire was in the basement."*

If the Chief had not ordered the evacuation, he and five of his Firefighters would have perished. How did the Chief know to evacuate the building? His intuition told him that something was wrong. His intuition told him to pull back and reevaluate the situation.

By using an Eisenhower Matrix

This method provides a framework for deciding which tasks to approach first.

The Eisenhower Matrix is a simple technique to help you decide which tasks from your "To-Do List" to perform immediately, schedule for later, delegate, or delete.

- **Urgent tasks** are things you need to react to, like emails, phone calls, texts, and news stories.
- **Important tasks** are things that contribute to our long-term mission, values, and goals.

Using this decision matrix (below), separate the tasks from your *To-Do List* based on these four categories:

- Urgent and Important (Do it Now).
- Urgent and Not Important (Delegate it).
- Important, but Not Urgent (Decide when to do it).
- Not Important, Not Urgent (Dump it).

This technique forces you to make hard decisions and delete any task that does not achieve your mission or goals. The matrix helps you determine how you should spend your time each week and what you should do today?

Here is an example of an Eisenhower Matrix.

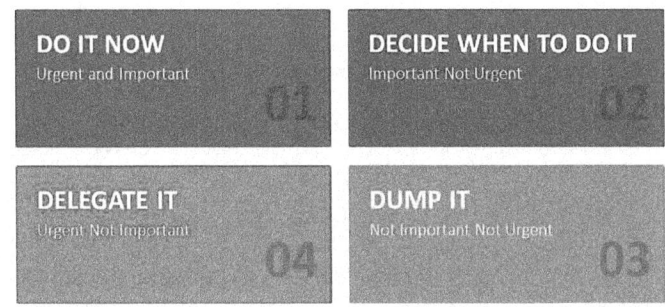

Too often, productivity and time management are used as an excuse to avoid the real question, *"What's the best use of my time right now?"*

By using the Red Team-Blue Team Technique

Effective people use every tool available when it comes to making the best possible decision. The role of the Blue Team is to use the *Problem-Solving Process* (PSP) to solve a problem for the boss. The role of the Red Team can vary depending on the boss's needs. The Red Team could play the role of instructor or evaluator.

Playing Evaluator means ensuring the other team uses the Problem-Solving Process correctly to select the Best Option.

The boss has three choices as to how to use this technique:

- He can ask both teams to work independently, and each presents their solution.

- He can ask the Red Team to sit in with Blue Team at the end of each step to play *Evaluator.*

- He can ask the Red Team to stay with the Blue Team throughout the process of playing *Evaluator.*

Playing Evaluator means ensuring the other team:

- Creates a good Problem Statement.

- Uses Creative Thinking and Critical Reasoning.

- Vets their facts and tests their assumptions.

- Identifies all possible options.

- Uses the Common-Sense Test to test all possible options.

- Creates good Screening and Evaluative Criteria.

- Uses Weighting Criteria correctly.

- Creates a good Raw-Data Matrix.

- Uses a Weighted Decision Matrix to create the Final Decision Matrix.

- Uses all the Problem-Solving and Decision-Making Tools available to select the BEST Option.

- Achieves consensus with the team after each step.

6
BY USING
PREVENTIVE ACTIONS

"The policy of being too cautious is the greatest risk of all."
- Jawaharlal Nehru

How do you find problems, or do you wait until they find you? Do you know how to uncover and resolve anything that could slow or stop your work?

Preventive Actions are all the things you should be doing 30, 60, or 90 days before any project to uncover all Pre-Problems.

This process is designed to find and correct any Pre-Problems before they get in front of your boss or the customer.

Pre-Problems include mistakes, defects, shortfalls, omissions, errors, or anything else that could slow or stop your work.

Here are the 20 most important *Preventive Actions* that should be added to your *Project's Timetable*.

THE PLANNING PHASE

1. Conduct an initial Site Inspection:

Visit the site to see if it meets your requirements. If you're asked to select the best site, visit several sites and present the best to your boss. Gather sufficient information (like photos, dimensions, and sketch maps) to help you create your *Draft Plan of Action* (Appendix A) and Appendix A) and prepare for your *Backbriefing* (Chapter 12). When picking the best site, the most important issues are location, availability, accessibility, cost, and amenities.

2. Create a Draft Plan of Action (POA):

This is your project **Plan of Action* (POA) that includes an Objective, Methods, Risk, Timetable, Resources Needed, and Unresolved Issues (Chapter 2 and Appendix A).

*To learn more about **Planning**, available at **Amazon.com,** see page 5.

3. Identify and eliminate all Unresolved Issues:

What are all the questions, unknowns, concerns, shortfalls, obstacles, or problems (*Unresolved Issues*) that could slow or stop our progress (Chapter 9)? Each issue can only be eliminated when it's both "*known for certain*" and "*acceptable to you.*"

4. Anticipate the Unintended Consequences:

What are all the adverse outcomes that aren't expected by your actions (Chapter 10)? Work hard to find anyone who has done this or a similar project before. What problems, consequences, and effects did they have?

5. Anticipate the Second and Third-Order Effects:

How could your project or decision affect others at different levels in your company (Chapter 10)? Work hard to find anyone who has done this or a similar project before. What problems, consequences, and effects did they have?

6. Conduct a Risk Assessment:

With your team's help, assess the risk of any safety, security, financial, and operational risks associated with the project and how they can be mitigated (Chapter 18).

7. Conduct a Backbriefing:

This is a briefing given by the Project Manager to his boss explaining how he intends to accomplish his boss's objective. This briefing enhances mutual understanding and trust by exchanging questions and answers to identify unmet expectations or hidden surprises (Chapter 12). Brief your boss using the *Plan of Action Checklist* (Chapter 2). Then, set the schedule for periodic *Project Updates* (Chapter 23).

8. Create a Memorandum of Record:

Finally, create a memo documenting the questions and answers from the *Backbriefing* and any questions you couldn't answer. Ensure your boss and all Key Players get a copy. A Key Player is anyone who must perform a task for a project to achieve its objective.

9. Provide Advanced Warning:

This is informing all Key Players of what's coming, so they can plan. Provide a copy of your Draft POA and the memo from the *Backbriefing* to each Key Player (Chapter 15).

10. Create Contingency Plans:

This plan is executed only if something bad happens that was anticipated, like bad weather (Chapter 21).

11. Staff the POA:

Circulate your POA through all Key Players for their concurrence or non-concurrence with comments (Chapter 16)

Conduct a Decision Briefing: Optional

Conduct a final briefing to the Decision Maker, with all Key Players present, to obtain final approval, if needed (Appendix B).

12. Conduct In-Progress Review (IPR 1):

Conduct at least two meetings before your project to synchronize all Key Players (Chapter 22). IPR 1 should be conducted at the mid-point of the time remaining between the Planning and Preparation Phases.

THE PREPARATION PHASE

13. Conduct Project Update Briefings:

Conduct a briefing to your boss summarizing the status of your project (Chapter 23).

14. Prepare to take Immediate Action:

This is a disciplined drill used to react to bad situations that could cause a work stoppage, property or equipment damage, a security breach, or physical injury (Appendix F).

15. Conduct a Final Site Inspection:

Conduct a last inspection of the project site to see if anything has changed since the initial inspection.

16. Conduct In-Progress Review (IPR 2):

This is a second (or final) meeting conducted 5 to 7-days before the project to confirm that all assigned tasks have been completed as planned (Chapter 22) between the Preparation and Execution Phases. This is when the rehearsal schedule should be distributed.

17. Conduct Rehearsals:

This is your last chance to see, practice, or test everything before the project to identify and correct any *Pre-Problems* (Chapters 6 and 25).

18. Conduct Pre-Staging:

This is the storage of equipment and supplies at the site before a project to make setup easier.

19. Conduct Site Set up:

Set up your site as planned. Having a site diagram (with extra copies) is a good idea – showing where everything goes.

Project Starts:

Supervise all Key Players to ensure the project achieves the desired objective. If problems arise, either execute *Immediate Action* (Appendix F) or a *Contingency Plan* (Chapter 21) to keep the project moving.

Conduct Site Clearing:

This includes all the actions taken after a project. The site may need to be cleared quickly to allow the next user to come in and stage their equipment.

THE ASSESSING PHASE

The Assessing Phase is conducted continuously throughout the project and is formalized using at least two *In-Progress Reviews* (or IPRs), several Project Updates (not shown), and an *After-Action Review* (or AAR).

20. Conduct an After-Action Review (AAR):

Conduct an informal meeting at the end of every project day (Chapter 26) and the day after the project with all Key Players present to focus on what happened vs. what was supposed to happen. Ask, *"What did we learn that can make us better next time?"* Add the *Lessons Learned* to the *After-Action Report.*

Conduct Project Close-out:

This includes all close-out details, like administering surveys, paying bills, sending letters, filing the *After-Action Report*, and other details.

7

BY USING A
PROJECT TIMETABLE

Time and tide wait for no man."
- Geoffrey Chaucer

Do you know how to ensure you've identified all important tasks, their proper sequence, and who's responsible for each? Your *Project's Timetable* should contain all the *Preventive Actions* needed to manage your next project.

Here's an example of a partial project timetable.

Partial Timetable for Company Picnic (June 21)							
Yr	M	D	Time	Preventive Action	Responsible	Where	Who
14	5	2	1 PM	Site visit conducted	Bob	B	1
14	5	4	2 PM	Backbriefing	Bob	A	2

Notice that this table shows the date, time, the *Preventive Action*, the person responsible, the location, who else is involved, and the correct sequence for each action.

The sequence is important because **Murphy's Law** states that:

> **"Whenever attempting to do anything, there are always things you should have done first."**

What did you forget (Appendix D)?

Which *Preventive Actions* will you add to your *Project's Timetable* to catch all the *Pre-Problems* before your project starts?

What if you don't know the dates yet?

Here's an example:

Bob was having lunch with Joe (one of his Direct Reports) and asked about an important project for his boss. Joe said, "I'll start working on the POA when the company decides on a start date." Bob asked him why he was waiting. Joe responded, "How can I write a POA when I don't know when the project starts?"

*Bob was stunned! He told Joe that the project starts every year in April, and today was January 1ˢᵗ, so he only had three months to plan. After lunch, Bob guided him through the creation of a Timetable using **S-Day as the Start Date**. Bob also asked Joe to add the most appropriate Preventive Actions to his Timetable.*

Here's an example of Joe's partial *Timetable*.

Partial Timetable for _____ Project (as of Date)							
Yr.	M	D	Time	Preventive Actions	Responsible	Where	Who
15	4	S-7	TBA	Final IPR	Joe	A	2
15	4	S-2	TBA	Rehearsals	Joe	A	2
15	4	S-1	TBA	Equipment pre-staged	Sam	B	2
15	4	S-Day	TBA	Project Starts	Joe	B	1
15	4	S+1	TBA	After Action Review	Joe	A	2

Notice that this timetable uses **S-Dates** instead of calendar dates because the project's start date has not yet been announced.

Joe then created a POA around this Timetable and began the Planning Phase. He labeled anything in the POA he didn't know for certain as TBA: To Be Announced. He then provided Advance Warning to all Key Players by giving them a copy of his draft POA. When the actual start day was announced, he plugged in the dates, notified all Key Players, and continued the Preparation Phase. If Joe had waited until the date was announced, several Key Players would have been in the last-minute crisis management mode.

Note: In the absence of instructions, make the assumptions needed to move the work forward (Appendix C).

If you fail to include *Preventive Actions* in your *Project's Timetable*, expect to experience the adverse effects of *Murphy's Law*.

8
BY USING AN
ASSESSMENT SYSTEM

"Don't tell your problems to people: eighty percent don't care, and the other twenty percent are glad you have them."
- Lou Holtz

How do you find problems, or do you wait for them to find you?

An Assessment System is a combination of targeted, proactive procedures designed to identify problems before they occur and resolve problems once identified.

This system is called CAPA (Corrective Actions, Preventive Actions) and should be part of your overall Quality Management System (QMS) and includes procedures to prevent problems (PA) and procedures to correct problems (CA) once identified.

Mistakes or defects are not a problem if they're identified and resolved before your boss or customer discovers them.

By using Preventive Actions

Preventive Actions are a series of specific procedures designed to identify pre-problems before they get in front of your boss or the customer?

Pre-problems include anything that could slow or stop the achievement of your goals (Chapter 6). What procedures do you have to identify problems BEFORE they get in front of your boss or the customer?

- Do you have processes, procedures, tests, rehearsals, inspections, visits, or assessments?
- Do you need periodic inspections, rehearsals, visits, or assessments to catch defects and mistakes?
- Who's checking, and what are they checking?
- How often and to whom do they report?
- What do they do when a problem is identified?
- Who's checking the checker?

Corrective Actions are a series of specific procedures designed to respond to problems AFTER they've been identified.

What procedures do you have to correct problems after they've been identified?

What's the Essence of a Finding?

Here's a system to capture, track, and resolve problems:

- **Problem #2214:** for tracking.

- **Standard:** What is the standard?

- **Condition:** What problem was found or observed?

- **Cause:** What is the root cause of this problem?

- **Risk:** What's our Risk?

    ✓ *Impact:* How <u>serious</u> will this problem affect the project?

    ✓ *Probability:* How <u>likely</u> is this problem to happen?

- **Recommendation:** What needs to be done to mitigate or eliminate the root cause?
- **Action:**

    ✓ Who is the *Point of Contact (POC)* to find a solution?

    ✓ When and how is the report rendered?

    ✓ What's being done to correct the problem?

    ✓ What's the current situation – same or worse and why?

Remember, mistakes or defects are not a problem if they're identified and resolved before your boss or customer discovers them.

What do sports teams use?

The day after the game, they all watch the game video. They document and record what happened. Then, they review the entire game, play by play. Did each play accomplish its goal? Did every team member do their job? If not, what needs to be done to improve for the next game?

9

BY ELIMINATING
UNRESOLVED ISSUES

*"There are two ways of spreading light: to be
the candle or the mirror that reflects it."
- Edith Wharton*

Do you know how to identify and eliminate any uncertainty that could stop or slow your ability to consistently produce excellent results?

**An Unresolved Issue is any question, unknown,
concern, shortfall, obstacle, or problem that
could slow or stop your progress.**

Your mission is to hunt down and eliminate all the *Unresolved Issues* associated with your work. If you don't, **Murphy's Law** will surely ruin your day. Don't let this happen to you!

So, do yourself a favor. Identify and eliminate all your *Unresolved Issues* early on to avoid the frustration, mistakes, and potential failure that could result from not having your-act-together.

Here are the most important steps to eliminate all your *Unresolved Issues*.

Step 1. Identify all Issues.

To identify all your *Unresolved Issues*, seek good answers to these questions:

- What do we need to know but don't?

- What do we know for sure, but the answer is unsatisfactory or unacceptable?

- What are all things we need but don't have?

- What are all the questions, unknowns, concerns, shortfalls, obstacles, or problems that could slow or stop your progress?

- Who has done this type of work before, and what were their problems, consequences, and effects?

- What are we forgetting to do (Appendix D)?

Step 2. State each issue in one sentence.

Each *Unresolved Issue* should be stated in one sentence and answer these questions:

- What do we need specifically?

- How much (or how many) do we need, exactly?

- Why do we need it - the purpose?

- When's the latest we need it?

- Where do we need it?

For example, let's assume that you're responsible for a *Team-Building Session* for your company, but you still need a guest speaker. So, your *Unresolved Issue* might read:

> **"Need to identify and contract one guest speaker for the final dinner, on June 23, at our annual Team-Building Session at the Hilton Hotel no later than June 1."**

Step 3. Add it to the Unresolved Issues List.

Here's a simple table for your *Unresolved Issues*.

Unresolved Issues List				
Date	Action Item	Who	Deadline	Status/ Date
May 4	Need to identify and contract one guest speaker for the final dinner, on June 23, at our annual Team-Building Session at the Hilton Hotel no later than June 1.	Tom	June 23	Ongoing /May 10

Notice that this table captures the date the issue was identified (May 4), the action item stated in one sentence, Tom is responsible for resolving the issue, the deadline (DL) is June 23, and the current status with the date you last checked is "Ongoing/May 10." The reason for this much detail is to enable your boss and his boss to help you resolve your issues without asking you any questions.

Step 4. Provide a copy to your boss.

Always ensure your boss has a current copy of all your *Unresolved Issues*. If he doesn't have these details, he can't help you.

Step 5. Continue to eliminate each issue.

All *Unresolved Issues* should go on your list until two things happen:

- Until the answer is *known for certain*, meaning that the answer is a fact rather than an opinion or speculation.

- Until the answer is *acceptable to you*, meaning that it's no longer an issue.

Keep the issue on your list until the issue is both **"Known for Certain"** and **"Acceptable to You."**

Don't be surprised when one issue is resolved that several new issues appear. Just add them to your list and get as much help as you can to resolve each issue.

Step 6. Seek Assistance.

Also, discuss your *Unresolved Issues* during any future meetings or updates. Others at the meeting may be able to help you - but they need to know your issues.

> *Look, this technique is designed to help you get things done. No one can help you if they don't know your Unresolved Issues. So, don't let your pride or fear get in your way.*

Always remember,

Asking for help is a sign of strength, not a sign of weakness.

Not knowing you need help is a sign of ignorance.

And needing help and not asking for it is a sign of stupidity.

So, don't get stuck on stupid!

When an issue is resolved, don't delete it from your list because you'll need it later for your *After-Action Review* (Chapter 26). Just record it as completed. When the issue is resolved, notify your boss.

Remember, the worst thing you could ever do is to conceal your Unresolved Issues from your boss.

This page is intentionally left blank.

10
BY ANTICIPATING
CONSEQUENCES AND EFFECTS

"The world is moved not only by the mighty shoves of heroes, but also by the aggregate of the tiny pushes of each honest worker."
- Helen Keller

Do you know how to anticipate and mitigate anything that could produce unexpected outcomes, causing delays or stoppage to your project?

By anticipating Unintended Consequences

Unintended Consequences are outcomes that aren't the outcomes expected from your project.

Unintended Consequences fall into three categories:

- **A positive**, unexpected benefit, which is usually referred to as serendipity or a windfall.

- **A negative**, unexpected problem like irrigation providing water for agriculture could also lead to cholera.

- The consequence of **what others might say or do** is referred to as backlash, fallout, or blowback.

Here's an example of negative *Unintended Consequences*.

Can you tell what's wrong with this picture? Hint: Does Starbucks really suck?

Answer: The painters applied the Starbucks advertising on a delivery van with the doors closed. Unfortunately, they failed to consider the unintended consequences of what the van would look like when the side door was open. This is *Murphy's Law* at its best!

By anticipating Second and Third-Order Effects

Be sensitive to how your work affects others.

Second and Third-Order Effects focus on how your work will affect others at different levels in your company.

Different levels mean how your work will affect others in your unit, department, company, and suppliers. *Second and Third-Order Effects* may also identify new resource requirements and cause changes to structures and procedures. For example, if you decide to change a supplier, the effects could be extensive.

- *Second-Order Effects* could require new ordering procedures to be created, which could cause delays.

- *Third-Order Effects* could require others to be retrained on new ordering procedures and software.

To anticipate *Second and Third-Order Effects* keep asking.

Now, what? What's next? What're we forgetting? And what could happen or what might we need to do in 30, 60, or 90 days?

How can you Anticipate Anything?

You're responsible for anticipating the consequences and effects of your work before starting.

But how can you do this when your crystal ball is no less clear than mine?

Method 1: Find others who have dealt with similar problems and ask:

- What problems, consequences, or effects did you have?

- Did everything go as planned? Any do-overs or surprises?

- What outside help did you need, and where did you get it?

- Anything or anyone you didn't have before starting?

- What was the most important and the most challenging task?

- How long did each task take, and what was the cost?

- Anything you'd start, stop, or change next time?

- Was everyone satisfied with the results?

Method 2: Vendors and Suppliers.

Contact vendors and suppliers who have worked with those who have dealt with the same or similar problems and ask the questions from Method 1. Also, which city, county, or state agency must inspect the issue to see if it meets the code?

Method 3: YouTube and social media.

Visit *YouTube* to search for related videos of others who have dealt with the same or similar problems. Then, get on social media and find people who have experienced projects or problems similar to yours. If you find someone, ask the questions from Method 1.

By making changes with CAUTION

Whenever a change is made, there are always consequences and effects. Just because everyone gets the change doesn't mean they understand it. The problem comes later when the consequences and effects start to appear, and everyone is shocked.

Here's a good example:

Bob was the Person-in-Charge of the company's Annual Team Building Session. Two days before the session, Bob's boss (the CFO) called and told him that the venue had been changed to a remote cabin where there was no electricity. Bob called John, the Key Player in-charge of food and beverages, to inform John of the change in venue and the lack of electricity.

The day before the session, Bob followed up with John and was shocked to find that John had not thought through the refrigeration requirements for the food and beverages. Since this was a three-day session, the change of venue not only required ice to be transported to the venue daily but coolers to store it.

John didn't recognize the need for ice, and Bob assumed John had it covered. As a result, the night before the session, both John and Bob spent several hours in the dark, scrambling around looking for coolers and bags of ice to fill them.

All this could have been avoided had John and Bob thought through the consequences and effects created by this last-minute change in venue by testing their assumptions and creating a Plan or Action to deal with it. Not to mention the need for a site recon and a review of the Checklist at Appendix D.

Murphy's Law on Consequences:

"There's never enough time to do it right, but there's always time to do it over."

11

BY

TAKING-CHARGE

When in doubt, mumble; when in trouble,
delegate; when in charge, ponder.
- James H. Boren

This chapter assumes that you've been assigned a project by your boss, and you're in the process of *taking-charge* as the Project Manager (PM).

Important Terms and Concepts

Backbriefing:

A briefing given by the Project Manager (PM) to his boss BEFORE starting a project, explaining how the PM intends to accomplish the boss's objective.

Being in-charge:

This means that you're the boss of a project (an assignment that requires the effort of others) assigned by your boss. Sometimes, your boss will make you the coordinator for a project. It could also be called the lead, point person, or facilitator. These are all ways of saying that you're *in-charge* with limitations.

When in-charge, take-charge!

Only your boss can tell you the extent of those limitations. If in doubt, ask! Make no assumptions. Do you have the authority to make decisions, task others, assign work, hire, fire, spend money, and set priorities? This is why you should always conduct a *Backbriefing* with your boss.

Boss:

The person you report to for your work assignments and pays you for your products and services.

Briefback:

A Q&A meeting called by the PM to ensure all participants understand the Plan of Action, their duties and responsibilities, consequences and effects, unresolved issues, and what to do when things go wrong.

Flexibility to Respond:

As the PM, you represent your boss in everything you do to ensure the project's success. However, you must retain your *Flexibility to Respond* because plans and projects rarely unfold as expected.

*Flexibility to Respond is your Freedom of Action
to check on your project, resolve problems, and remain
responsive to your members and your boss.*

This means always staying in contact with all participants and your boss, being free to roam and reposition your members, equipment, or supplies to where they're most needed. That means that you must delegate any problems or obstacles to another team member or Key Play so that you don't get diverted with ancillary issues causing you to take your eye off the big picture. Once you get bogged down as a doer, you're no longer the PM.

Effective PMs are in-motion checking and encouraging!

Key Player:

Anyone who must perform a task for your project to succeed doesn't report to you (like a vendor, supplier, or a member of a different department).

Project:

Any assignment that requires the effort of others to achieve the objective and includes achieving goals, resolving problems, and conducting activities or events.

Project Manager:

The person assigned by the boss to conduct a project: the *person-in-charge*.

Tasking Authority:

Your ability to assign work to another member. For example, you only have *tasking authority* over your direct reports, which are those members who report to you for their work assignments.

If they don't work for you, you have no *tasking authority*. However, your boss and his boss have *tasking authority* over many more members that can be assigned to you temporally to complete your project.

Team Member:

This includes anyone who normally reports to you for their work assignments, your Direct Reports.

By knowing what a Project Manager does

When In-charge, Take-charge!

What are the most important things a PM should do?

- Always protect your *Flexibility to Respond*.

- Step up and take responsibility and accountability for a project from start to finish (Appendix G).

- Ask questions, listen to concerns, pay attention, and delegate authority, but never responsibility.

- Build consensus with the team.

- Facilitate problem-solving and collaboration.

- Be willing to change the plan when needed, demonstrate flexibility, and adapt to changing conditions.

- When things go wrong, you own the mistakes. When things go well, you share the success.

- Be proactive and responsive by checking and making things happen!

- Provide a Backbriefing to your boss to ensure you understand his expectations.

What should a PM NOT do?

As the PM, you should NOT:

- Become engaged in physically helping a team member because it limits your *Flexibility to Respond* elsewhere.

- Attempt to resolve problems or unresolved issues. Delegate it to a team member.

Here's a Great Story

One day, John (the boss) visited a work site to check on a sub-project conducted by one of his Direct Reports (Bob). John asked Bob how things were going. Bob had two job sites as part of his sub-project.

John then visited Bob's second job site and saw that the members there were doing nothing. Bob's members tried to call Bob but got no answer. John tried to call Bob but got no response. Frustrated, John drove back to the first site and asked Bob why he wasn't answering his phone. Bob said his phone was in his truck.

John then pulled Bob aside for some on-the-job correcting and said, "Bob, I need you to have your phone with you at all times. Also, I just came from your second site and found that your team had no idea what they were supposed to do. I need you to get over there to straighten things out. Also, you need to check both your sites first thing every morning to ensure they get started the right way."

Bob lost his *Flexibility to Respond* because he left his phone in his truck, and no one could contact him.

Are you a Micro-Manager?

Well, let's see. The opposite of effective delegation is micromanagement.

Micromanagement is a management style whereby the boss closely observes and controls the work of a Direct Report.

Micromanagement also includes the suppression of constructive criticism that could otherwise lead to internal reform and job turnover. In micromanagement, the boss not only tells the Direct Report WHAT to do but dictates HOW to do it.

A frequent cause of micromanagement comes from the boss's doubt whether the Direct Report is competent enough to complete the project. Effective delegation requires a well-defined objective, a clear vision of the constraints and dependencies, and effective oversight.

So, are you a micro-manager? Do you trust your Direct Reports? Would they agree? Any room for improvement?

12
BY CONDUCTING A
BACKBRIEFING

"Progress always involves risks. You can't steal
second base and keep your foot on first."
- Frederick B. Wilcox

This chapter assumes that your boss assigned you as the Project Manager (PM) for an upcoming project. One way to ensure no unmet expectations and misunderstandings between you and your boss before your next project is to conduct a Backbriefing.

A Backbriefing is a briefing given by the Project Manager to his boss BEFORE starting a project, explaining how the PM intends to accomplish the boss's objective.

As far as your boss is concerned, if he assigned you to be the person-in-charge of an assignment - the assignment belongs to you – and you're the Project Manager (PM).

Backbriefings are an excellent way to achieve a "meeting of the minds" before work begins. They enhance mutual understanding and trust by exchanging questions and answers to ensure no unmet expectations or hidden surprises later. They benefit all parties by reducing misunderstandings and the need for rework. They also enhance your credibility, thus relieving the need for micromanagement.

When should a Backbriefing be conducted?

In business, there are two types of projects.

- **Expected Projects** are projects already part of your job description, like an annual trade show. For expected projects, provide a Backbriefing at least 90 days before the project.

- **Requested Projects** are newly assigned projects and should receive a Backbriefing a week after receiving the assignment.

Here are the most important steps to conduct a good Backbriefing:

Step 1. Conduct an Initial Site Inspection.

Visit the site to see if it meets the requirements. If you're asked to select the best site, visit several sites and present the best to your boss. Gather sufficient information (like photos, dimensions, and sketch maps) to help you create your Draft *Plan of Action* (Chapter 2 and Appendix A) and prepare for your *Backbriefing* (Chapter 12). The most important issues when picking the best site are location, availability, accessibility, and cost.

Step 2. Create your Draft Plan of Action.

Use the *Plan of Action* Checklist in (Chapter 2 and Appendix A) to create your draft.

Step 3. Identify and eliminate all Unresolved Issues.

An Unresolved Issue is any question, unknown, concern, shortfall, obstacle, or problem that could slow or stop your progress (Chapter 9).

Step 4. Anticipate the Consequences and Effects.

List any Unintended Consequences and Second and Third-Order Effects (Chapter 10). Work hard to find anyone who has done this or a similar work before. What problems, consequences, and effects did they have?

Step 5. Conduct a Risk Assessment.

Assess the risk of anything that could slow or stop your project or cause physical harm, security failures, and financial loss and how they can be mitigated (Chapter 18).

Step 6. Brief your boss using the Plan of Action Checklist (Chapter 2 and Appendix A).

You're not expected to have all the answers, but you're expected to have all the questions. So, as a minimum, obtain answers to these questions:

- What's the desired end-result or objective?
- How will success be measured?
- What are all the most important tasks that must be completed?
- Who's responsible for each major task?
- What's your authority to make decisions and spend money?

Then, set the schedule for periodic *Project Updates* (Chapter 23). Capture any new Unresolved Issues or questions your boss asked that you couldn't answer. If the boss doesn't want a Backbriefing, send him your draft POA and get his approval.

Step 7. Create a Memorandum of Record.

Finally, create a memo documenting what happened during the Backbriefing and any questions you couldn't answer. Ensure your boss and all Key Players get a copy. If you fail to conduct a Backbriefing with your boss before your next project, do so at your peril.

You've been WARNED!

This page is intentionally left blank.

13
BY MANAGING
A BUDGET

"The budget is not just a collection of numbers, but an expression of our values and aspirations."
- Jacob Lew

Is budgeting part of planning? You Bet! Effective people know that good planning includes good budgeting. Without good budgeting, you'll run the risk of running out of money before the end of the year. This will bring your business unit to a halt and make your boss very unhappy.

Many people shy away from certain positions because they fear budgeting - fear of the unknown. However, once you understand the basics of budgeting, you'll see how similar it is to manage your family's finances.

A budget is nothing more than an estimate or projection of what your proposed expenditures will be for next year.

How do you create an Operating Budget?

If you're a small business owner, your survival depends on your expenses not exceeding your revenues. This is where projections or estimates come to play, which are based on assumptions (Appendix C). Assumptions are needed to create your *Requirements*.

Requirements come from your boss and are what you and your business unit are required to do (and what it will cost) over 12 months.

The best way to start creating your budget is with the *Requirements*, which come from your boss. To accurately prepare your budget submission, you need your boss's goals and objectives for the next year and a schedule of known projects/events scheduled for the next year. Without these, you'll just be guessing.

These documents should come from your boss or your boss's boss. Now that you have your goals and objectives, counsel with your Direct Reports to determine your unit goals and objectives for the year and what it will cost for you to meet these goals and objectives. To come up with your listing of goals, objectives, and costs - look at last year's data, if available, and collaborate with your boss about their budgets.

How do you manage a Budget?

If you have *Profit and Loss* (P&L) responsibility (where you get to manage your budget), you're given a budget and have the authority to spend money to run your unit for 12 months. Budgets normally include salary, *training, trips, and scheduled events.

Your job is to expend these funds wisely without running out of money (going over-budget). Find out what costs are included in your budget from your CFO/Finance team. What fees do you pay, and what costs does your organization pay?

Let's assume you have a $500,000 budget. Subtract out 10% ($50,000) as a safety cushion to protect you if you have an unexpected expense during the year. This leaves you $450,000 to spend in the next 12-months. Subtract out the annual salaries for all your Direct Reports (if it's included in your budget).

Let's also assume you have 12-Direct Reports, and their total salary is $300,000. With other mandatory expenditures of $50,000, this now totals $350,000. This leaves $100,000 to spend over the next 12-months (or $8333.33/month) for monthly expenditures to run your unit.

Keep track of your monthly expenditures (minus salary and other mandatory items). Don't spend more than $8,333.33, on average, in any one month, without a good reason. This is your monthly limit.

Delegate this accounting task to a Direct Report and ask for an expenditure report at the end of every month. To spend over your budget limit requires your boss's approval. Watch out for unexpected expenditures. Set dollar limits for your Direct Reports. If you don't, you'll find yourself over-budget very quickly.

Why should you prioritize your budget line items?

In the real-world, you can't have everything. This is why you *prioritize*. Your boss may ask you to do more with less. This means a budget cut. If your budget gets cut 10%, what'll you cut from your budget? If you already have your budget line-items prioritized, from your highest to lowest priority, you'll be well prepared for any adjustments to your budget. So, how do you *prioritize*?

*To learn more about **Training**, available at **Amazon.com,** see page 5.

The first step is to look at all the things you have listed in your budget. Rank-order all your line items, with the most important (directly related to your goals) at the top. Next, sit down with your team to get their input. Do they agree with your rank-ordering? If not, why not? Finally, review your rank-ordering with your boss. Does your boss agree? If not, why? Adjust your rank-ordering as needed.

Everything you spend money on should be directly linked to your goals!

Why do you want to prioritize your budget? *Prioritizing* helps you prepare for budget-cutting. When this happens, it will now be much easier to determine where to make your cuts.

What about your requisitions?

Another budget-related task is tracking outstanding *Requisitions*. This task should be assigned (delegated) to one of your Direct Reports. Have your requests for a product or service left your organization yet? When is it due to arrive? Track these dates to ensure you receive what you requested.

What about unfinanced requirements?

Every year, you'll find things (that can help you better achieve your boss's goals) that you wish you had the budget money to purchase. When this happens, document the requirement, just in case there are extra year-end funds available for the purchase. If not, defer it to next year's budget.

What about end-of year funds?

Near the end of every year, when computing all the expenses, there may be additional funds available to use for unfinanced requirements.

This page is intentionally left blank.

14
BY ANTICIPATING
CHANGE

"It is not necessary to change. Survival is not mandatory."
– W. Edwards Deming

Change is ongoing, pervasive, and in most cases, is beyond your control. You can't stop it. Why not get good at welcoming it in such a way that it adds value to your career? By embracing change, you'll put yourself far ahead of your peers - who are still struggling against the inevitable. How can you do that? Here are the most important things you can do to embrace change.

By becoming more adaptable.

The perception of change is that it will require more work, cause you to be outside your Comfort Zone, or make you look stupid by learning something new. The only constant in life is change. Most people don't realize that staying in their Comfort Zone is the formula for mediocrity and professional stagnation.

This is why in business, you have only two choices:

either adapt or perish.

This is the *Theory of Natural Selection, Darwin's Theory of Evolution.* Adaptability, one of the nine most influential character traits, is the ability to recognize changes in the environment, identify the critical elements of the new situation, and trigger changes accordingly to meet new requirements or situations. Effective people consider multiple perspectives, don't jump to conclusions, are teachable, recognize a change in the environment, are constant learners, identify the critical elements of a new situation, trigger change accordingly to meet new requirements, and effectively change their behavior in response to an altered situation.

By building consensus with the team (Chapter 16).

By providing Project Updates.

By providing *Project Updates* (Chapter 23) to your boss and requiring the same from your team members, you're putting yourself in a far better position to respond to change.

By staying connected to your boss and Key Players.

Without a good *Unanticipated Situation Plan* (Chapter 21), you'll quickly find yourself running around trying to put out fires that belong to your *Key Players* - who are away from or not answering their phone.

By preparing to take Immediate Action.

Since projects, no matter how simple, rarely unfold as expected, be prepared to take *Immediate Action* by assessing the situation and issuing new instructions to respond to the changes (Appendix F).

By assessing and mitigating risk.

Without having good *Contingency Plans* prepared, you can guarantee being stopped by last-minute changes over which you have no control (Chapter 19).

By tracking all changes.

By tracking all the changes that occur, you're capturing and disseminating information that could otherwise cause your assignment to fail (Appendix E). Also, you'll need a list of all changes for future meetings. Always ask, *"Who else needs to know this change?"*

By ensuring everyone understands the effects of the change on them.

Just because everyone received your changes doesn't mean they understand how the change affects them.

Here's a good example:

"Bob was the Person-in-Charge of the upcoming Team Building Session for his company. Two weeks before the session, the CEO changed the venue to a remote cabin with no electricity. Bob immediately informed John (the Key Player in-charge of Food and Beverage) of the new venue and the lack of electricity. The day before the session, Bob followed up with John and was shocked to find that John had not thought through the consequences and effects of the change on the refrigeration requirement. Bob assumed that John would take care of it, and John assumed that Bob had done it. Unfortunately, the venue change required ice to be transported to the remote venue and coolers to store it. As a result, both John and Bob had to scramble around in the dark looking for coolers and bags of ice to fill them. All this could have been avoided had John and Bob thought through the consequences and effects the change had on their assignments."

15

BY PROVIDING
ADVANCED WARNING

"History is a vast early warning system."
- Norman Cousins

Do you know how to provide important information to your team members and Key Players to ensure they know what you're planning and have sufficient time to prepare?

How would you feel if your boss just told you that
you're flying to Europe tomorrow when he's
known about it for a month?

A Key Player is anyone you're counting on to perform a task for your project to be a success.

Advanced Warning is informing all team members and Key Players of what you're planning, so they can plan.

The most important thing you can do for your team members and Key Players is to give them as much time as possible to plan and prepare by telling them what you're planning to do. You do this by providing as much Advanced Warning as you can.

In the **US Military**, it's called a *"Warning Order,"* and it includes an Objective statement from the Draft *Plan of Action* (POA) telling as many specifics as possible. It should also include the who, what, when, where, and why.

Unless the task is time-sensitive, an email to each team member and Key Player should suffice. However, provide as much information as you can. If anything is unknown, list it as TBA (To Be Announced).

What's the "One-Third, Two-Thirds Rule?"

When planning a project, the rule states that if there are three weeks until a project starts, the first week is yours to create the Plan of Action and Backbrief your boss, and the two remaining weeks belong to your Key Players for their planning and preparation.

This page is intentionally left blank.

16

BY BUILDING
CONSENSUS WITH A TEAM

"Unity is strength... when there is teamwork and collaboration,
wonderful things can be achieved."
- Mattie Stepanek

Do you know how to achieve agreement from all team members that they can support a proposal? Few people in the workforce today understand the meaning and value of collaborating to build consensus.

The process of building consensus starts with collaboration.

> **Collaboration is the process of working with others**
> **to resolve a problem or achieve a goal.**

Building consensus results from collaboration. Most people think that consensus means that everyone must like the proposal, the majority rules, or some other lame criteria - all of which are false.

Here's the truth!

> **Consensus is the desired end-product of**
> **collaboration intended to achieve agreement from all**
> **team members that they can support a proposal.**

> **Support means that each member agrees that**
> **the proposal will work and commits to doing**
> **all they can to ensure its success.**

If not, this is their chance to speak up! The process of building consensus gives every member the freedom to voice their agreements or disagreements before consensus is achieved. It's also intended to be inclusive, participatory, and cooperative, seeking opinions and input from all members.

Consensus uses common agreement to resolve mutually exclusive positions. It's not the majority rules, nor a popularity contest. It doesn't care whose proposal is being considered or if any member likes or dislikes the proposal. It only asks each member if they can support the proposal. If not, a valid reason must be provided.

**VALID means that their reason must be either a
better proposal or a fact and not an opinion.**

Why is building consensus important?

To answer this question, I always ask,

What's the Greatest Hunger of the Human Heart?

What does every human being need to be fulfilled at work?

*The Greatest Hunger of the Human Heart
is to be NEEDED.*

To be needed means:

- To be seen means to be included and validated.

- To be heard means to be listened to, understood, and appreciated.

- To be valued means to be recognized for their contributions.

- To be treated with respect and kindness because they matter.

*The greatest hunger of the human heart is to
be seen, heard, valued, and treated with respect
and kindness because they matter.*

If team members aren't allowed to *"speak their piece,"* you're telling them that they're not important and they don't matter. Not good! Do you feel needed where you work? Do those who work with you feel needed? Do you treat everyone with respect and kindness-no matter what?

*Everyone needs to be engaged, involved, and have a say
concerning the things that affect their wellbeing.*

This is why consensus building is so powerful.

When's consensus needed?

Consensus is needed whenever you're trying to resolve a problem, create a plan, or make any change that affects the team.

What are the benefits of building consensus?

- Consensus building improves the proposal by using the wisdom and knowledge of the team.

- It uncovers any Unintended Consequences and Second and Third-Order Effects that could slow or stop the proposal.

- It builds trust and commitment from the team by engaging them and using their input.

Building consensus is far more important than achieving it because, in the end, everyone may not agree to support the proposal, but at least they've been included in the process.

Failure to build consensus will erode teamwork, commitment and cause the failure to consistently produce excellent results. Building consensus sounds easy, but it's not. However, it's worth it because, without their involvement, they'll never be committed! And without their commitment, you'll never be able to consistently produce excellent results!

By building Consensus

Here are two methods of building consensus:

- **Staffing a Proposal.** This means circulating a proposal document through all team members to obtain their concurrence or non-concurrence with comments.
- **Conducting a Team Meeting.** This method works best when the proposal is an important decision that's time-sensitive, involves major funding, and affects the entire team.

If this is the case, here are the most important steps to build consensus.

Step 1. Discuss the proposal.

Gather the team, either at one location or on a phone or video conference and discuss the proposal.

- **If the proposal is a problem,** how was it discovered, how bad is it, and what're the risks if it continues unresolved? What's causing this problem? Is this the real problem or just a symptom? And how do we know for sure?

- **If the proposal is a goal,** why is it important? What's the intended benefit?

Step 2. Discuss the Solution.

If the solution is obvious, then work with the team to create the *Plan of Action* to implement the solution. If there could be several solutions, conduct a *Brainstorming Session* and select the best solution (Chapter 21).

Step 3. Anticipate the Consequences and Effects.

Once the solution has been identified, discuss the possible *Unintended Consequences* and *Second and Third-Order Effects* (Chapter 11).

Step 4. Eliminate all Unresolved Issues.

Discuss and identify all *Unresolved Issues* (any question, unknown, concern, shortfall, obstacle, or problem) that could slow or stop your progress (Chapter 10).

Step 5. Ask for Consensus.

Now, ask all team members if they can support the proposal. If not, why? Remember,

> **Support means that each member agrees that the proposal will work and commits to doing all they can to ensure its success.**

If all members agree, ask them to create the *Plan of Action* to implement the proposed solution. If any member has a valid reason for non-support, continue to Step 6.

By resolving Reasons for Non-Support

At this point, only valid reasons should be considered. However, real-life doesn't work that way. Members will always have concerns and opinions, and they need to be heard. Here are the most important steps.

Step 6. Deal with their concerns.

If a member has a concern or opinion that's not a fact, this is when things get interesting.

- If their concern is that it's **too costly**, what does he mean? Too costly compared to what? How can the cost be reduced or offset? What's the contingency plan if it does cost more?

- If their concern is that it **will take much longer**, what's he basing this on? What's the downside if it does take longer? What's our Contingency Plan if it does?

- If their concern is that it's **too risky**, what does he mean? Can it be mitigated? Can a contingency plan be created just in case?

Step 7. Convert Reasons to Risks.

Before continuing, exchange the term *"Reason"* for *"Risk."* This will make this process much easier to understand. And for each risk, there are two critical things you must consider, probability and impact.

Step 8. What's the Probability?

How likely is this risk to happen (Chapter 12)? If the probability is *Low*, place the risk, *On-Hold*. This means that it's been noted and set aside temporarily. If the probability is *Medium* to *High*, or you're unsure, continue to the next step.

Step 9. What's the Impact?

What's the Impact or Effect on the proposal when this risk happens (Chapter 12)? If the Impact is *Minor,* place the risk *On-Hold*. If the Impact is *Moderate* to *Significant*, or you're unsure, continue to Step10.

Step 10. Can the Risk be Mitigated?

- If the risk can be mitigated, create a *Contingency Plan* (Chapter 15).
- If the risk can't be mitigated, you still have three options (Chapter 14).

Remember, you don't need a consensus before sending the proposal to your boss for approval. However, you'll need to include all reasons for non-support and let your boss decide. All members don't have to like the solution! They just need to be able to support it.

Here's another method of building consensus without a meeting.

Staffing is the process of circulating a proposal document to all team members to obtain their concurrence or non-concurrence with comments in writing.

This method works best in situations where the proposal is routine and not time-sensitive. The proposal document could be a procedure, plan, question, or idea. Here are the four most important steps.

Step 1. Provide the proposal document to all members.

Ensure each team member receives a copy of the proposal document. Ask each member for their concurrence or non-concurrence with comments. And don't forget to provide a deadline.

Step 2. Resolve non-concur comments.

When member comments are returned to you, you may need to visit some members privately to better understand their comments and determine if adjusting your proposal could lead to their concurrence. Remember, concurrence means that each member agrees that:

The proposal will work and commits to doing all they can to ensure its success.

If not, a valid reason must be provided, which means their non-concur comments must be a better proposal or a fact and not an opinion.

Step 3. Make changes.

If you need to make changes, you'll need to send the revised proposal to all members again for another review. And for the second review, ensure you highlight any changes made from the first review.

Step 4. Obtain approval.

Note: You don't need the concurrence of all team members before sending your proposal to your boss for approval, but you'll need their reasons for non-concurrence. Remember, building consensus should never be done in a vacuum. You need the feedback to help you see beyond your blind spots.

17
BY MANAGING RISKS

There is only one big risk you should avoid at all costs, and that is the risk of doing nothing."
- Denis Waitley

Do you know how to manage the risks associated with your work?

Simply Stated, RISK is Uncertainty!

Managing anything requires the ability to anticipate and mitigate risk. You can't control everything that happens to you, but you can control your degree of preparation and how you respond.

Here are the most important things to consider when assessing risk.

1. Reduce the Risk of Failure.

By planning for risk to occur, you're decreasing your probability of failure, which increases your probability of success. Much of this is done every day in your company. It's called risk reduction, like having fire, theft, and liability insurance.

2. Understand that control is an illusion.

This simple prayer, which I learned during my recovery from alcoholism, helped me finally answer this life-altering question:

What are the only things in life I can control and therefore change?

THE SERENITY PRAYER
"God, grant me the Serenity to

Accept the things I cannot change,

Courage to change the things I can,

and the Wisdom to know the difference

- Reinhold Niebuhr

And these answers changed my life forever.

**In this life,
You cannot control or change other people,
places, things, situations, or circumstances.**

**The only things you can control and therefore
change are your thoughts, words, and deeds.**

And all those years, I thought I could control and change other people. What a waste of time and energy. This may come as a shocking epiphany for many of you because you've probably made the same mistake.

*Yes, you can influence them, but you can't control
or change them. You can only control
and therefore change yourself.*

This concept is crucial because until you learn to truly control what you can control (your thoughts, words, and deeds), you'll never influence anyone to help you consistently produce excellent results.

3. Identify your Risk Goals.

When it comes to managing risk, you should always have two goals.

- Make the Risk LESS likely to happen, like putting training wheels on your child's bicycle.

- Make the Impact LESS severe when, and NOT if it happens, like requiring your child to wear a safety helmet.

4. Plan for both Anticipated and Unanticipated Risk.

In life, there are always two categories of risk:

- *Anticipated Risks* are those risks that include all the things that could *reasonably-go-wrong*, including anything that could slow or stop your project or cause injury, illness, accident, death, security violations, property damage, or financial loss.

- *Unanticipated Risks* are those Risks that you could not possibly have predicted (Chapter 21).

5. Conduct a Risk Assessment.

With the help of your team, conduct a *Risk Assessment*. What are all the things that could *reasonably-go-wrong* (Chapter 18)?

Anticipated Risk comes in two forms:

Bad Internal Situations are things that don't require a call to 911, like equipment breakdowns, people being late, cell phone batteries going dead, and other mistakes, defects, or errors.

Bad External Situations are things that will require a call to 911, like fire, injuries, accidents, property damage, violence, or theft.

6. Assess the Impact and Probability.

For each Bad Situation, assess these two critical things:

Impact means how this Bad Situation will affect your project and is rated as *Significant, Moderate, or Minor*. Based on your assessment, when, and not if, this Bad Situation happens, how serious will it affect your project?

Probability means how likely is this Bad Situation to happen and is rated as *High, Medium, or Low*. Based on your assessment, how likely is this Bad Situation to occur?

7. Assess your Risk Options.

Option 1. AVOID the Risk.

In some cases, you may want to avoid the risk altogether. This could mean not getting involved or just deleting a high-risk activity. This is a good option when taking the risk involves no advantage or when the cost of mitigating isn't worth the risk. However, when you avoid a potential risk entirely, you may miss an opportunity. So, do your *What if Analysis* to explore your options before deciding. To learn more, search *YouTube* for *"What if analysis on Excel."*

Option 2. SHARE the Risk!

You could decide to share the risk and the potential gain with others. For example, you share risks when you insure your project site or partner with another company.

Option 3. ACCEPT the Risk.

This option is usually best under these conditions:

- When there's nothing you can do to prevent the risk.

- When the potential loss is less than the cost of insuring against the risk.

- When the potential gain is worth accepting the risk.

For example, you might accept the risk of a project launching late if the potential sales will still cover your costs.

8. Beware of Scope Creep.

Scope means the size of the project and its requirements, complexity, and goals. Scope creep occurs when others want to make changes to your project. So, negotiate these changes to gain either more time or more money, or both.

9. Create Contingency Plans.

The purpose of any *Contingency Plan* (Chapter 21) is to diminish the severity of a bad situation when it occurs. *Contingency Plans* need to be *Staffed* (Chapter 16) through all Key Players and approved by the boss.

10. Use Preventive Actions.

Mistakes are not a problem if they're caught before they get in front of your boss or the customer.

What *Assessment Systems* (Chapter 8) or procedures do you have to catch mistakes? Effective people anticipate and mitigate their risk by adding *Preventive Actions* to their *Project's Timetable* (Chapter 7).

18

BY CONDUCTING A
RISK ASSESSMENT

"Take risks: if you win, you will be happy; if you lose, you will be wise."
- Unknown

Effective people know that conducting a good *Risk Assessment* is critical to their probability of success. You can't control everything that happens to you, but you can control your degree of preparation and how you respond. With the help of your team, conduct a good *Risk Assessment* by *Brainstorming* (Chapter 20) anything related to your work that could *reasonably-go-wrong.*

Here are the most important steps to conduct a good *Risk Assessment.*

Step 1. Anticipate the Physical Risks.

Have you inspected the site for anything that could cause an injury, accident, illness, or death? How about safety, sanitation, and access for those with disabilities - any risk there?

Step 2. Anticipate the Security Risks.

- For *cybersecurity*, what could cause a data breach, personal info or intellectual property loss, or a disruption of services?

- For *physical security*, what could permit unauthorized access leading to theft or property damage?

Step 3. Anticipate the Financial Risk.

- What could cause financial loss through fraud, waste, or abuse?

- What insurance is needed, and is it current?

Step 4. Anticipate the Operational Risks.

- What's the *Impact* when these risks occur (Chapter 17)?

- What's the *Probability* these risks will happen (Chapter 17)

- How can these risks be mitigated (Chapter 19)?

- What's your *Contingency Plan* for when they do (Chapter 21)?

- Do your team members know how to take *Immediate Action* (Appendix F)?

- What assumptions are needed to move the work forward (Appendix C)?

- What *Preventive Actions* did you add to your *Plan of Action* (Appendix A) and *Timetable* (Chapter 7)?

- Have you *Staffed* your POA (Chapter 16) with the team, and what was the result?

- What are you forgetting to do (Appendices D)?

Step 5. Eliminate Unresolved Issues.

What are all the questions, unknowns, concerns, shortfalls, obstacles, or problems that could slow or stop our progress (Chapter 9)?

Step 6. Anticipate and Mitigate Unintended Consequences.

Unintended Consequences are the outcomes that aren't expected by your actions (Chapter 10).

Step 7. Anticipate Second and Third-Order Effects.

Second and Third-Order Effects focus on how your recommendations or decisions affect others at different levels in your organization (Chapter 10).

Step 8. Anticipate the Risk of Bad Situations.

Bad Internal Situations are situations that *don't require a call to 911*, like equipment breakdowns, people being late, cell phone batteries going dead, mistakes, defects, or errors.

Bad External Situations are situations that *require a call to 911*, like fire, injuries, accidents, property damage, violence, or theft (Chapter 19). If you fail to conduct a good *Risk Assessment* before your next project, do so at your peril.

You've been WARNED!

19
BY MITIGATING THE RISK
TO BAD SITUATIONS

"If you are not living on the edge, you are taking up too much room."
- Jayne Howard

To manage anything, you need to know how to mitigate your risk. In business, there are two different types of risk:

By mitigating the Risk to Bad Internal Situations

This includes equipment breakdowns, people being late, cell phone batteries going dead, and other mistakes, defects, or errors.

Bad Internal Situations are situations that don't require a call to 911.

Once you've determined everything that could *reasonably-go-wrong*, you're ready to mitigate the risks. Here are the most important steps.

Step 1. Brainstorm.

Conduct a *Brainstorming Session* to determine what actions are needed to respond to each bad situation (Appendix K).

Step 2. Create Contingency Plans.

Now that you've determined what actions are needed for each Bad Internal Situation, it's time to create a *CONPLAN* for each (Chapter 21).

Step 3. Rehearse each CONPLAN.

Rehearse each *CONPLAN* a few days before your project to identify any errors, omissions, or misunderstandings. Don't just ask people if they're ready. Ask them to show you that they're ready (Chapter 25).

Step 4. Eliminate All Unresolved Issues.

Continue to eliminate all *Unresolved Issues* by facilitating collaborative problem-solving to build consensus (Chapter 9).

The truth is that even though local first responders have more resources and training than you, you can still make the risk less likely to happen and make the impact less severe when it occurs.

Bad External Situations are those that require a call to 911.

Here are the most important steps to mitigate the risk of Bad External Situations.

Step 1. Assess the Risk of Fire.

Since most fires start as small fires, do you have more fire extinguishers on-site than you need? Do people know where they're located and how to use them? Have they been tested and inspected? Are there sufficient smoke detectors present and serviceable? Are there any local restrictions on burning, building fires, or fire warnings?

Step 2. Assess the Risk of Medical Issues.

Do you have first aid kits on-site, with staff trained on how to administer first aid? When were these kits last inspected and replenished? Can ambulances be located closer to your venue? Do you have staff trained to administer CPR? Do defibrillators be centrally located with staff trained in how to use them?

What about those who have food allergies and those allergic to bee stings? And how about mosquitos, the elderly, and the disabled? Are there any unsafe conditions that could lead to an injury or accident? Are there any unsanitary conditions that could lead to illness?

Step 3. Assess the Risk of Crime.

Whenever assessing the risk of crime, always consider:

- **Access control** means entry denial, metal detectors, gates, locks, keys, fences, barriers, checkpoints, firewalls, passwords, and badges.

- **Deterrence** means cameras, guards, dogs, signs, security lighting, punishment for violators, and barbed wire.

- **Early warning** means alarms, security systems, loudspeakers, intercom, flashing lights, police alerts, lockdowns, and sirens.

20
BY CONDUCTING A
BRAINSTORMING SESSION

"To win without risk is to triumph without glory."
- Pierre Corneille

How many times have you just assumed that you knew the BEST solution to a problem, only to find out later that you were wrong? Effective people understand the value of *Brainstorming* when resolving problems and achieving goals.

Brainstorming is a group process of producing the most potential options to resolve a problem or achieve a goal.

Here are the most important steps.

Step 1. Pick your team.

Keep your group small (seven or less). If more than seven members, break them into smaller groups and compare the results.

Step 2. Use Mindstorming (Optional).

The day before, give each team member a sealed envelope with instructions not to open it until they get home that night. Inside the envelope are instructions to conduct a *Mindstorming Exercise* by writing down many potential problems' options. Also, ask them not to share their options before the meeting the next day.

Step 3. Prepare needed materials.

You'll need a blackboard, whiteboard, or some large sheets of paper on a vertical easel, wide-tipped markers to record all options for all to see.

Step 4. Decide how you'll participate.

Some members may not feel comfortable if you conduct the session. If you ever feel that your presence could diminish the team's effectiveness, find something else to do.

Step 5. Assign other duties.

If needed, select someone else to facilitate the *Brainstorming Session* and assign another member to act as the *Scribe* to record each option.

Step 6. Conduct the meeting.

A good *Brainstorming Session* should consist of these three phases:

Phase I. Capture All Options:

Limit this phase to 10-15 minutes or just enough time for each member to present their options. In this phase, you're looking for volume only. Judgment or criticism is reserved for the next phase.

Phase II. Discuss all Options:

After capturing everyone's options, this phase is where discussion is encouraged and options are consolidated.

Phase III. Validate each Option by using the "Common-Sense Test:"

This phase is designed to assess the validity of each option by using the *Common-Sense Test.* This test asks five questions about each option to qualify it as a valid option. If any option receives a *"No"* or *"we're not sure"* answer, it's eliminated.

1. Is it Suitable? Does the option solve the problem, and is it legal and ethical?

2. Is it Feasible? Does it fit within available or easily acquirable resources?

3. Is it Acceptable? Is it worth the cost and the risk?

4. Is it Distinguishable? Does it differ significantly from other options?

5. Is it Complete? Does it solve the problem from start to finish?

Step 7. Select the Best.

In the end, you should have a list of valid options that require further research to help you select the best option. *Brainstorming* helps build commitment. Since you've included the team in the selection process, they'll be more committed when the time comes to implement the best option.

Involvement builds commitment, and commitment is critical to the consistent production of excellent results.

21
BY CREATING
CONTINGENCY PLANS

"If you don't risk anything you risk even more."
- Erica Jong

Do you know how to create a plan to respond to anticipated bad situations?

By creating a Contingency Plan

Have you ever been involved with a project when things went wrong? What did you do? Was there a *Contingency Plan,* and was it rehearsed*?*

A Contingency Plan (or CONPLAN) is a Plan of Action that assumes that an anticipated bad situation has occurred.

A *CONPLAN* is only executed when something bad happens. Being prepared is the key! What's your plan? Remember,

Many bad situations never become a problem

because someone knew what to do and had

the resources to respond.

Here are the most important steps:

Step 1. Collaborate.

Once you've identified all the bad things that could *reasonably-go-wrong,* collaborate with your team to determine what actions should be taken in response.

Step 2. Assess the Impact.

Impact means how this Bad Situation will affect your project and is rated as *Significant, Moderate, or Minor.* Based on your assessment, when, and not if, this Bad Situation happens, how serious will it affect your project?

Step 3. Assess the Probability.

Probability means how likely is this Bad Situation to happen and is rated as *High, Medium, or Low*. Based on your assessment, how likely is this Bad Situation to occur? If you have a bad situation with a Significant Impact and a High Probability of occurring, you'll need lots of help.

Step 4. Create a CONPLAN.

Once you've identified the actions that should be taken, create a CONPLAN to deal with each Bad Situation. Each CONPLAN uses the same format as a *Plan of Action* (Appendix A) but begins with assumptions. This assumption is the Bad Situation that you and your team have already anticipated. Your CONPLAN tells the reader exactly what to do when the assumption becomes false. It also lists what's needed, where it's stored, and how to use it.

Let's assume that you were assigned as the Project Manager for your company's *Team Building Session* in Buffalo, NY, in January. You and your team have already anticipated three Bad Internal Situations that could *reasonably-go-wrong* with your project.

You assessed the Impact to be Significant for guests arriving late because the Team Building Session won't be effective without all guests. However, you estimated your probability to be *Medium* because of the weather in Buffalo this time of year. So, for guests arriving late, you intend to use CONPLAN A.

> **For transporting guests to the resort:** You estimated the Impact to be *Moderate* because of the weather, the fact that the resort is 27 miles away, and that delays will disrupt the success of the team building session. And you assessed the probability to be *Medium* because you know that the weather in Buffalo this time of year is always a challenge. So, for Transporting guests to the resort, you intend to use CONPLAN B.

> **For lost baggage:** You estimated the Impact to be Minor for lost baggage because your activity can still go on regardless. However, you estimated the Probability to be *High* because the airlines have a history of losing luggage in the winter. So, for lost baggage, you intend to use CONPLAN C.

Step 5. Create your Risk Matrix, and here's an example.

Risk Matrix for Team Building Session			
BAD SITUATION	**IMPACT**	**PROBABILITY**	**CONPLAN**
Guests Arriving Late	Significant (8-10)	Medium (4-7)	A
Transport to Resort	Moderate (4-7)	Medium (4-7)	B
Lost Baggage	Minor (1-3)	High (8-10)	C

Notice that this simple table shows all Bad Internal Situations, their Impact, Probability, and which CONPLAN to use. The risk numbers 1 - 10 are used to help create your *Risk Threshold*.

Step 7. Staff your CONPLANs.

Staff your CONPLANs through all Key Players for their concurrence or non-concurrence with comments (Chapter 16).

Step 6. Assess your Risk Threshold.

Here's an example of a *Risk Threshold Table*.

Risk Threshold = Impact X Probability.		
Risk Rating	**Risk Range**	**Remarks**
CRITICAL	50 or higher	The acceptable risk threshold for safety and health should always be lower than your financial or operational risks.
MEDIUM	16 to 49	
LOW	15 or Lower	

Notice that this table shows that a *risk threshold*, rated from critical to medium to low, is the sum of the impact times the probability. Knowing your risk threshold is important because your acceptable safety and health risk threshold should always be lower than your financial or operational risks. Ideally, you should be doing all you can to reduce your risk. And if you can't, you'll need a good CONPLAN ready to respond.

Step 8. Obtain Approval.

Present your CONPLANs to your boss for approval with all the comments from your Key Players attached.

Step 9. Distribute your CONPLANs.

Once approved, ensure that all Key Players have a copy of all CONPLANs well before the project starts.

Step 10. Rehearse your CONPLANs.

A few days before your project starts, rehearse your CONPLANs with all Key Players (Chapter 25).

By creating an Unanticipated Situation Plan

Do you know how to create a plan to respond to unanticipated bad situations?

An Unanticipated Situation Plan (or USP) is a Contingency Plan that assumes that an unanticipated bad situation will occur.

When unanticipated bad situations occur, what do you do? Is that even possible? Preparing for *Unanticipated Bad Situations* requires a different level of thinking and preparation. Regardless of how well you plan, you'll always encounter bad situations that you did not, nor could not have anticipated. So, what do you do?

As a Project Manager, what will you do when an *Unanticipated Bad Situation* occurs on your watch? Your boss is counting on you to do everything you can to save, salvage, or secure your project.

You can't control everything that happens to you.
But you can control your degree of preparation
and how you respond.

You already know that many Bad Situations never become problems because someone responded to them swiftly and decisively. They had *Assessment Systems* (Chapter 8) and people in place to respond to these situations when they occurred. They saved the day!

But how did they do it? They did it by creating an *Unanticipated Situation Plan,* a *Contingency Plan* that focuses on *Unanticipated Risk.*

Here are three special techniques that will help you prepare for and respond to *Unanticipated Bad Situations*.

1. Create a Quick Response Team (or QRT).

A *QRT* is a team specifically trained and equipped (with vehicle, keys, access codes, cash, and credit cards) on *Stand-by* (they have no other duties and are ready to respond, 24/7). Provide a sketch map to all *QRT* members that shows all locations near or at the site as reference points.

2. Use a Priority Response System.

The system is a cellphone protocol that requires that all Key Players:

- Respond to their cell phone before the <u>second</u> ring.
- Have extra batteries and car chargers readily available.
- Carry their cell phone on their person 24/7.
- Never let incoming calls from you go to voicemail.
- Have all contact numbers of all Key Players on their phones.
- Limit their outgoing calls to ensure they're able to respond.

This system is only effective if everyone plays by these rules. This is why it should be rehearsed. When you call, you need the Key Player to answer before the <u>second</u> ring - no excuses.

3. Create a Pre-Stocking Site.

This site is stocked with any materials, equipment, and supplies that could cause a delay or stoppage of your project.

- Do you have backup bulbs, projectors, and extension cords?
- Do you have backup batteries and AC and DC chargers?
- Where will these items be located?
- Do your boss and all Key Players know this location?

Have one trusted Key Player responsible for this site, ready to deliver what, when, and where it's needed. Also, this site could be mobile, like a van or truck pre-positioned at or near the site, as needed.

Always be prepared to take *Immediate Action* (Appendix F).

No one likes being on a project when things are going badly. So, how can you get the project back *on track*?

A *Mitigation Plan* is a POA designed to get a project back on track by eliminating, consolidating, or rescheduling certain tasks to finish close to the originally planned date.

Here are the most important questions to ask if you ever have a project in trouble:

- Are there any tasks that can be eliminated, combined, or compressed?

- Is there **Slack Time* that can be used?

- Can anything be done simultaneously (or done *off-line*)?

- Do you need more people? Can overtime help?

- Should you go to a second shift or run 24-hours?

- Can working on the weekend and holidays help?

- Can the scope (size, requirements, complexity, goals) be reduced?

- Can the end time be moved to allow a successful completion?

---

*Slack time: The amount of time in a schedule that a task can be delayed without causing a delay to other tasks or the project's completion date.

Getting behind schedule isn't fun. How does any project get thirty days behind? Answer: one day at a time, repeated thirty times. So, what's the message here? Don't get behind in the first place!

For those of you who think you'll never have to create a *Mitigation Plan* in your lifetime, think again. If you have a plan for getting your college education, MBA, or a Ph.D., what happens if you must take a year off? It's called a *Mitigation Plan* to help you pick up the pieces and move forward.

22
BY CONDUCTING AN
IN-PROGRESS REVIEW

"If I had to live my life again, I'd make the same mistakes, only sooner."
- Tallulah Bankhead.

Do you know how to determine if your project is progressing as planned and if it's ready to move to its next phase?

An In-Progress Review is a synchronization meeting conducted by the Project Manager with all Key Players present to collaborate and coordinate a project.

Normally, each major project will have at least two *IPRs* scheduled between phases of the project.

IPR 1 is normally scheduled at the halfway point of the time remaining (between the Planning and Preparation Phases).

IPR 2, the second or last IPR, is normally scheduled 5-7 days before the project starts (between the Preparation and the Execution Phases).

IPRs essentially become *Milestones* (A tool used to mark specific points along a project timeline and focus on major progress phases that must be reached before moving forward).

What should be discussed during each IPR?

If this is your project, this is your opportunity to check if everyone involved, especially the *Key Players,* are on-schedule, knows about all changes, and has no *Unresolved Issues* (Chapter 9).

Deliverables: During the IPR, the project's current progress is addressed, and *deliverables* designated in the *POA* are presented. A *deliverable* is something tangible that proves that a Key Player has taken action specified in the *POA* (like a sales receipt, a purchase order, or diagram). If all *deliverables* are present, the project moves to the next phase. If all *deliverables* are not presented, the project is stopped (or delayed) until the boss becomes directly involved for explanations and gives the go-ahead.

Unintended Consequences and Second and third-Order Effects (Chapter 10).

Unresolved Issues (Chapter 9).

23

BY CONDUCTING A
PROJECT UPDATE

*"It takes half your life before you discover
life is a do-it-yourself project."
- Napoleon Hill*

Do you know how to provide important information to your boss concerning the current status of your projects to ensure he understands your progress, changes, and *Unresolved Issues?*

A Project Update is a summary of a project provided to the boss and all Key Players as to the status of a project.

Your boss may have some changes or modifications to the original *Plan of Action* (Appendix A). These last-minute changes are usually the things that complicate any project. So, prepare for these changes, document them carefully, and communicate them to all Key Players. There are two ways to provide a *Project Update*, either by a Briefing or a Dashboard.

By conducting a Project Update Briefing

Here are the most important steps.

Step 1: Overall assessment.

When reporting the summary, give the *bottom-line*, *up-front*. Then, justify your assessment. How's the assignment doing in relation to the scope, schedule, money, and people from the original POA?

Positive assessments: On-schedule, within budget, looking good, progressing nicely.

Negative assessments: Behind-schedule, in trouble, over-budget, or has major problems.

Step 2: Unresolved Issues.

Present any question, unknown, concern, shortfall, obstacle, or problem that could slow or stop your progress (Chapter 9). If new problems are introduced, the boss will expect you to present options to resolve these problems and recommend which option is best. Your boss will also expect you to have already given the problem to all Key Players for their concurrence or non-concurrence with comments (Chapter 16).

Step 3: Changes.

Present any new changes since your last briefing.

Step 4: Close.

Close by summarizing and restating any assignments made during the briefing or any Follow-through action. Confirm the date and time of the next update. Prepare a Memorandum for Record (MFR) to document what happened during the meeting.

By creating a Project Update Dashboard

The most popular type of business dashboard is the Google Analytics Dashboards, used on 55% of all websites, which shows the activity on a website, like visits, entry pages, bounce rate, and traffic sources.

A Dashboard is a graphic or picture providing at-a-glance views or "snap-shots" of Key Performance Indicators relevant to a project's objective or a business process.

It's posted where all Key Players can access it (like a shared-drive so all can check progress, 24/7). Here's an example of a Dashboard.

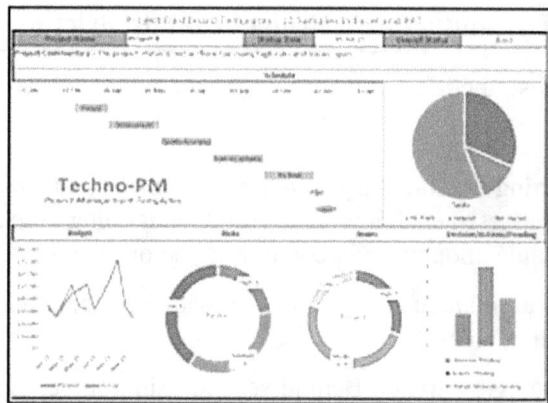

If done manually, ensure you update it every week or as changes occur. Email any changes to all concerned. Since a Dashboard is intended to provide the same material as a Project Update Briefing, design it to quickly give the same important information. You can also add links to other documents, like Frequently Asked Questions (FAQ).

24
BY MAKING
CHANGES TO A PROJECT

"Without change there is no innovation, creativity, or incentive for improvement. Those who initiate change will have a better opportunity to manage the change that is inevitable."
- William Pollard

Do you know how to make changes to a project to ensure nothing *falls-through-the-crack?* Last-minute changes will happen, and problems will suddenly appear, so expect it. After distributing the POA, determine the cost and consequences of making this change if changes are needed. Then, ensure your boss approves the change. Any POA is only good until the first few minutes of any project's execution. From then on, make any necessary adjustments to achieve the desired end-state while keeping all *Key Players* informed.

Adjustments (or changes) in the **US Military** are called FRAGO's (or *Fragmentation Orders*). In football, they're called *Audibles*. They are both last-minute changes to the plan normally caused by changes in the situation or conditions. If you're the boss, this is what's required during the Execution Phase. So, prepare for it. Just make sure all your *Key Players* get the word on all the changes.

What are the most important things to do when giving Change Instructions?

- Make it clear who is assigned to take action, including the Who, What, When, Where, How, and Why.

- Document and track who received each change (so people can't say I never got the change).

- If time-sensitive, speak face-to-face (or on the phone), then *Follow-through* via email or hard-copy.

- *Follow through* later, ensuring everyone got the change and understood the consequences and effects.

- Ask another to review the change document before it's sent.

- Send it to everyone who needs to know.

- Who did you forget (Appendix D)?

Most important to understand is that many bad situations don't become a problem unless you don't know what to do or don't have what you need to deal with the situation.

Why do things get worse AFTER you make a change?

Caution: When you make a change in response to a bad situation, often things get worse because of two reasons:

First, a *Key Player* was not informed (I didn't get the memo). This is why you track the date, the person who received the change, and the delivery method.

Second, after a *Key Player* receives the change, he does not fully understand the consequences and effects. This is where he may need your help.

25
BY CONDUCTING A
REHEARSAL

"Take calculated risks. That is quite different from being rash."
- George S. Patton

Do you know how to uncover and correct any pre-problems that could slow or stop your project?

By Rehearsing

A Rehearsal is the process of reviewing (looking at) the results of others before they get in front of your boss to ensure all Pre-Problems (mistakes, defects, shortfalls, omissions, or errors) have been resolved.

The type of rehearsal I'm referring to here is to examine everything concerning your project BEFORE your boss sees it. How hard is that?

Why do you think weddings have rehearsals?

Do you have the ring, know where to stand, know what to say, and know the sequence of what's going to happen next? And why does it matter? Who wants it to be perfect? Enough said. What do you need to see, test, or practice a few days before your project starts?

Get a Clue! Even criminals have rehearsals because they know the consequences if they don't.

Rehearsals include things like previews, layouts, practice, a sand-table, or white-board walk-throughs. They also include demonstrations, role-playing, document reviews, and testing. And when your rehearsal uncovers a flaw, have it fixed and have another rehearsal.

Caution! Never ask people, *"are you ready?"* Instead, say, *"Show me that you're ready. I want to see it!"* What's stopping you?

Look, I can't tell you how many times I've been burned by people who've said to me that they were ready when they weren't. So, do yourself a favor. If this is your project, your job is to check. That means looking at everything before it gets in front of your boss.

By Practicing

As a child, I was told that *"Practice makes perfect."* As an adult, I learned that this was false. It should be,

"Perfect practice makes perfect."

If you're practicing the wrong way, your results will suffer. That's why you always need a coach, someone who can show you how it should be done correctly to achieve the best result.

My favorite practice quote comes from **Coach Paul *"Bear"* Bryant**.

> ***"It's not the will to win that matters – everyone has that.
> It's the will to prepare (or practice) to win that matters."***

It's no wonder **Coach Bryant** amassed six national championships and thirteen conference championships as the head coach of the University of Alabama's football team.

Growing up, I also learned that to be the best, I needed to *"Practice until I got it right."* However, much later in life, I found that to master anything, I needed to

"Practice until I couldn't get it wrong."

The best example of this comes from **Mary Lou Retton**, who won the gold medal in the 1984 Olympics in LA. She scored a perfect 10 in the vault competition.

After that vault, she asked the judges if she could do it again to show it wasn't just a lucky vault. Her score was another perfect 10. More impressive was that she was a sophomore in high school, had recently had leg surgery, and won two silver medals and two bronze medals. Her performance was historic because she was the first-ever American woman to win the all-around gold medal at the Olympics, making her the most popular athlete in the US.

26
BY CONDUCTING AN
AFTER-ACTION REVIEW

"We don't have a crisis of leadership in Washington.
We have a crisis of followership."
- Jonathan Rauch

How can you enhance your performance and the performance of your team? One way is to use *After-Action Reviews.*

An After-Action Review (AAR) is a professional discussion conducted after an activity, with all members present, seeking ways to consistently improve the way things are done.

AARs should be conducted both during (at the end of each day) and the day after an activity (project, objective, or goal) by measuring the difference between what was supposed to happen (the Plan) vs. what did happen (Behavior and Results). Thus, AARs observe, measure, record, and assess an activity or process from start to finish to examine the results and the behavior of those involved.

The purpose of an AAR is to:

- Capture and share intuition by asking HOW and WHY questions.

- Attempt to discover WHY things happen and how to get better.

- Help members understand HOW and WHY decisions are made.

- Encourage members to become *self-correcting* and more *aware of how their behavior affects others (Appendix G).

- Capture *Lessons Learned* to integrate into future operations.

Here are the four most important steps to conducting an AAR:

Step 1. The Objective.

Before the activity (project, objective, or goal): What are we trying to achieve? What performance standards and results are desired? Who and what will be observed, and how will it be measured?

*To learn more about *Awareness*, available at **Amazon.com,** see page 5.

Step 2. The Results and Behavior.

During the activity: What happened? What was observed and measured? What are the facts?

Step 3. The Assessment.

After the activity: Did things go as expected? Were there any surprises? If the result wasn't what we expected, what should be started, stopped, or changed to achieve a better result? WHY and HOW did we do what we did?

Step 4. The Lessons Learned.

What did we learn that can help us do better next time?

By using Informal After-Action Reviews

Let's assume that you're the Project Manager for a four-day Trade Show and you have three team members.

The week before the show, you and your boss sat down to discuss the plan and its objective. Why are we attending this show? What's the ideal outcome you'd like to see? How will this outcome be measured? After finishing with your boss, you met with your team and briefed them on the plan. Fast forward to the end of the first day of the show. You assembled your team and asked, what did we learn today that can make us better tomorrow?

One team member said it would have been nice to have some bottled water in our booth. A second member said, we also need a lunch schedule, so everyone has a chance to eat. Also, we're running low on our advertising brochures. You then asked one team member to provide bottled water in the booth every day. Then you asked another member to set up a lunch schedule for each day. And finally, you called your boss and asked him to overnight a bunch of advertising brochures. You also conducted an informal review at the end of each day with the goal of continuous improvement.

The day after the trade show, you gathered your team together and asked if we accomplished our goal? Did everything go as planned? Were there any surprises? What did we learn that could make the next Trade Show better? You then added all comments to your After-Action Report so next year's Trade Show can be even better. How hard was that?

27
BY CONTRIBUTING TO
THE BOSS'S MEETINGS

"It is the responsibility of leadership to provide opportunity,
and the responsibility of individuals to contribute.
- William Pollard

Do you know what you need to do and not do during your boss's meetings because this may be the only contact your boss has to observe your performance? These meetings will be attended by your boss's other Direct Reports - your Peers. So, get to know them. Help them in any way you can.

Why do bosses conduct meetings?

- To learn what's going on concerning the status of assigned work.
- To pass on what he knows about what's important to his boss.
- To monitor the team's efforts to move the work forward.

What are the most important things to do during these meetings?

- Arrive 15 minutes early to get to know your Peers.
- Display respect and kindness.
- Demonstrate support for your boss by your 100% attention, involvement, and participation.
- Put your cell phone on vibrate or leave it outside.
- Support for your peers. *Teamwork is critical.
- Come with the attitude to contribute, encourage, and help others.
- Demonstrate an understanding of your boss's goals.
- If you cannot attend, send someone to discuss your agenda items and *Unresolved Issues* (Chapter 9).
- And if you have no one to send, call your boss the day before and provide your update.
- To wait for others to finish before speaking.
- To follow up with answers to questions you couldn't answer.

*To learn more about **Motivation**, available at **Amazon.com,** see page 5.

What are the most important things not to do during these meetings?

- Hog the air-time. Be brief and let others speak.

- Wander off the agenda. Help your boss keep others on track.

- Surprise your boss. Bosses hate surprises - unless it's great news.

- Interrupt or cut someone off. If you must, then apologize!

- Embarrass or surprise a peer.

- Find fault or complain. Only do so privately with your boss.

- Continue arguing after the boss has made his decision?

- Ask a question that could embarrass someone. Ask it privately.

- Be late or absent without calling.

If you fail to understand and meet these expectations, you'll never be considered a *Team Player*.

What's the bottom-line on Communicating?

Good communication isn't about you - it's about them!

Do they understand what you want them to do? And how do you know for sure? You won't unless you ask! And whose responsible and accountable if they didn't understand and the project goes bad?

To be considered effective or essential by any boss, you must be perceived as someone who can be counted on to excel at two things:

- To consistently produce excellent results.

- To add value to all those who helped produce those results, especially the boss.

Your ability to communicate will play a huge role in that assessment.

Get your *act together, or your credibility will suffer!

*To learn more about **Organizing**, available at **Amazon.com,** see page 5.

28
BY GIVING AND
RECEIVING FEEDBACK

"Feedback is the Breakfast of Champions"
- Ken Blanchard

Do you know how to enhance your effectiveness and the effectiveness of those with whom you work?

Feedback is information about a member's performance, which is used as a basis for improvement.

The goal of feedback is to identify the gap between <u>desired</u> and <u>actual</u> performance (for results and behavior) of members, teams, units, and systems) and to close the gap ASAP.

Feedback can occur anytime but normally comes during audits, performance-oriented training, performance appraisals and reviews, shareholders' meetings, marketing research, 360-degree feedback, peak performance coaching, visits and observations, on-site inspections, surveys, meetings, and *After-Action Reviews*.

What's the Feedback Loop for Human Performance?

Here are the most important steps of the *Feedback Loop*.

Step 1: Evidence: The performance must be measured, recorded, and assessed.

Step 2: Relevance: Feedback must be relayed to the member in a context that makes sense.

Step 3: Consequence: Feedback must illuminate a path to improvement.

Step 4: Action: Members must change their <u>actual</u> performance to come closer to the <u>desired</u> performance.

Then, that new performance can be re-measured, and the feedback loop can run once more, every action stimulating new performance that moves the member closer to the <u>desired</u> performance.

By giving Feedback

If you fail to provide periodic and specific feedback to your members, your silence will speak louder than words. It's your job to let them know how they're doing.

- If your feedback is **positive**, share it with everyone publicly.

- If your feedback is **negative** or a correction (like someone failed to meet a standard), do so privately. Take a moment to ensure the member knew the correct standard and didn't have a good reason for doing (or failing to do) what he did.

However, giving someone your opinion doesn't constitute feedback unless they act on your opinion and thus cause you to revise your opinion.

By receiving Feedback

When you receive feedback, you get to decide how you'll respond and if you'll use it to become more effective. Feedback is often perceived as a euphemism for criticism. If you just "blow it off," you'll never get any better. You don't have to agree. Initially, you won't. However, arguing or being defensive sends the wrong message.

If you don't receive feedback, ask for it, not only from your boss but from others.

Humble yourself! Remember, you need the feedback, no matter how painful, because you'll never become more effective or successful without it. Also, the person giving the feedback might someday be in a position to shape your future.

So, be *self-correcting*! Prove that you're listening and getting better every day (Appendix G).

Effective people thrive on feedback because their goal is to become more effective and successful.

Is it your job to provide feedback to your boss? Absolutely! You owe it to your boss. But how do you do it?

Providing feedback to your boss takes moral courage and is the most challenging part of being loyal to your boss; telling him what he doesn't want to hear - like the TRUTH.

Feedback is normally defined as information that you privately provide to someone intended to improve their performance. However, when it comes to your boss, it's a little more complicated. When giving feedback to your boss, your intent must be perceived as being done to help him stay out of trouble, avoid, or correct a mistake, resolve problems, achieve goals, and look good in the eyes of his boss.

As such, here are the most important steps:

Step 1. Set the stage.

This means that whatever you have to say must be done privately. You might even suggest that you and your boss take a walk to somewhere private where you won't be interrupted.

Step 2. Gain permission.

If you've not already done so, ask and receive confirmation that you have permission, to be honest.

Step 3. Preface your remarks.

Preface your remarks by saying, *"I need to give you some feedback on…"* or *"I just wanted to tell you how I feel about…."* or *"I just thought you needed to know…"*

Step 4. Deliver your message.

Speak your peace and remind your boss of why you're saying what you did.

What happens if your boss gets angry? This could happen - no big deal. You're not there to blow smoke up his butt. You're there to make him and his unit better tomorrow than they are today. Period!

What if I get fired? My response is, Great! You're the lucky one! You no longer have to work for a jerk who fails to appreciate your loyalty for telling the truth.

Privately providing honest feedback to your boss is the stronger half of courage and loyalty.

When was the last time you took your boss for a walk and discussed what was going on?

Caution: There is a fine line between tattling and reporting the facts. Tattling is done to get someone in trouble. Feedback is done to either keep him out of trouble, help him achieve his goals, or to make him look good in the eyes of his boss. When you tell your boss about a mistake he made or is about to make, you're doing so to keep him out of trouble. Do you have good communication with your boss? If not, why? If in doubt, ask!

Remember, the only stupid question is the one you're too afraid to ask. Because, later, when you don't know the answer, you'll look stupid or worse!

Note: As a new member, during your first 90-days, you can ask any question you want, and no one will care. After that, they'll be wondering why they hired you!

29

BY CONDUCTING
INTERNAL MEETINGS

Murphy's Law on Meetings:
A meeting is an event at which the minutes
are kept, and the hours are lost.

Do you know how to conduct productive and meaningful meetings to enhance the quality and effectiveness of your team?

Have you ever been to a meeting that was a waste of time, and you just wanted to leave? Was it your meeting? Today, many face-to-face, sit-down meetings are often unproductive, especially when considering all the advanced communication technology available. However, meetings can be productive and meaningful, and here are a few suggestions.

1. Simplify your Agenda.

Most meetings I've attended failed to get to the heart of the problems needing attention.

Here are the most important components:

Present: What are you currently working on, and when do you expect to finish?

Future: What are you planning to accomplish before our next meeting?

Unresolved Issues: Do you have any questions, unknowns, concerns, shortfalls, obstacles, or problems that could slow or stop your progress (Chapter 9)?

After starting the meeting, go around the room and ask everyone to comment on their three agenda items. You may even request that everyone submit their three agenda items via email to you or the meeting facilitator the day before. This way, a copy of each person's response can be provided to all participants at the meeting.

2. Preside instead of conduct.

Ask someone else to conduct your meeting so that you can preside. Conducting a meeting is good training for your #2 person. It allows you to observe the body language, note who's not participating, and inject, clarifies, question, reinforce, or redirect, as needed.

3. Hold members accountable (Appendix G).

In a non-threatening way, *accountability* means asking:

- How are you progressing on your assignments?
- How do you intend to resolve your problems?
- Do you need more time or other resources?

If someone needs more time to complete a task, consider renegotiating a new deadline (Appendix E).

4. Don't get distracted.

The reason for not dealing with new, non-emergency, *Unresolved Issues* is to avoid being distracted and losing focus during your meeting. If a new *Unresolved Issue* is brought up, that's a non-emergency and can't be resolved quickly; you have several options.

- Assign someone to lead another meeting to resolve the issue. Assign all others that you feel need to be at that meeting.
- Assign the person who brought up the issue to write a *Decision Paper* (Appendix B).
- Assign the person who brought up the issue to come to see you with a recommended solution before the next meeting.

Most importantly, don't leave this issue without an assignment. Near the end of the meeting, review all assignments made during the meeting.

5. Consider setting these expectations.

- Meetings start and end on time and last no more than one hour.
- If you can't attend, send someone to discuss your agenda items.
- Bad language isn't permitted, and only one person speaks at a time.
- No throwing anyone *under-the-bus*, especially if not present.
- Do everything you can to support each other (Teamwork is critical).
- No distractions, no texting or *communicating on any devices.
- I expect your 100% attention, involvement, and participation.
- I expect you to treat everyone with respect and kindness
- Come to participate, contribute, encourage, and help others.

*To learn more about **Communicating**, available at **Amazon.com,** see page 5.

30
BY BUILDING
TRUST

"Better to trust the man who is frequently in error
than the one who is never in doubt."
- Eric Sevareid

Trust is the glue that holds everything together for any company. Trust is important in business because it forms the basis of all relationships and interactions.

Trust is the firm belief in the reliability, honesty, integrity, ability, or strength of someone.

Creating a sense of trust is the most important factor when considering team member performance. Successful businesses are built on relationships, and the foundation of all relationships is trust. Unfortunately, there may be times when some people may not see eye to eye.

However, if members treat each other with respect and kindness and can get their ideas across without feeling belittled or discriminated against, then trust can be built. Without trust, your ability to come to an agreement or build consensus will always be compromised.

What are the benefits of trust?

- Increases productivity and improves morale.

- Enables members to work more effectively as a team.

- Reduces the time needed to discuss key issues and make decisions.

- Facilitates cooperation and collaborative *problem-solving.

- Improves effectiveness and diminishes costs.

- Expands teamwork and sustainability.

Trust is the emotional component of companionship, friendship, love, agreement, relaxation, and comfort.

*To learn more about *Problem-Solving*, available at **Amazon.com,** see page 5.

Why are some bosses reluctant to delegate?

The main phobia bosses have about delegating is losing control. I get it. However, the truth is that you never had control in the first place.

Control over other people is an illusion!
But, influence through persuasion is achievable.

The sooner you realize this fact, the quicker you'll achieve order from chaos and let others do their job. The key to delegating is to do so gradually until you know who can move the work forward and who can't.

Are there different degrees of trust?

Here's a list showing the different degrees of trust, starting with showing *very little trust* and ending with showing *complete trust*:

- Bring the facts to me for action (little trust).

- Develop alternatives, and I'll take action based on the facts.

- Be prepared to take action, but don't do anything until I say so.

- Tell me what you propose to do and when.

- Analyze the situation, take action, and tell me the results.

- Just go! Here's the situation; deal with it! (complete trust).

How do you build trust?

Do you know the most important components of building relationships? You shouldn't be surprised that it's trust. How much does your boss trust you? How much trust do you have in your team members?

Here are the important components of building trust:

- If others sense that you're AUTHENTIC, you're much more likely to be trusted.

- If others sense that your LOGIC is solid, you're far more likely to be trusted.

- If others sense your EMPATHY is sincere and directed at them, you're far more likely to be trusted.

When all three are present, you have their trust. But if any one of these three is missing or needs work, trust is in question.

How can you become more Authentic?

In human relations, your lack of authenticity is considered bad faith in dealing with other people.

Authenticity is the degree to which your actions are congruent with your beliefs and desires, despite external pressures to conform.

You'll tend to hold back who you are for fear that someone might dislike you. You may even go so far as to be more like those with whom you work, hoping to fit in. Unfortunately, all this only makes you less likely to be trusted.

Pay less attention to what other people think about you and more attention to what you think about yourself. We all have an obligation to set and maintain the conditions that not only make it safe to be authentic but make it welcome. It's the key to achieving greater effectiveness.

How do you do it? You do it by being yourself and treating everyone with respect and kindness.

How can you enhance your Logic?

Logic is the study of correct reasoning, especially as it involves the drawing of inferences.

Logic has two gates that you must pass through to be acceptable.

- It must be rational, reasonable, and doable.
- It must be communicated in a manner that's easily understood, straightforward, and supported with evidence.

How can you show Empathy?

Empathy is the capacity to understand or feel what another person is experiencing and the capacity to place oneself in another's position.

There are two levels of empathy:

Cognitive empathy means that you're capable of understanding other people's thoughts and feelings.

Affective empathy, in addition to understanding, means that you're capable of feeling other people's emotions and of sharing their grief, suffering, and joy.

In addition to creating trust, these three skills can help you build an emotional connection with others and genuinely relate to their feelings. Empathy can be learned to help bring you closer to having greater success in your relationships.

Are you a Micro-Manager?

Well, let's see. The opposite of effective delegation is micromanagement, where a manager gives too much input, direction, and review.

Micromanagement is a management style whereby the boss closely observes and controls the work of a Direct Report.

Micromanagement also includes the suppression of constructive criticism leads to job turnover. In micromanagement, the boss not only tells the Direct Report WHAT to do but dictates HOW to do it.

A frequent cause of micromanagement comes from the boss's doubt whether the Direct Report is competent enough to complete the project successfully. Effective delegation requires a well-defined objective, a clear vision of the constraints and dependencies, and effective oversight.

So, are you a micro-manager? Do you trust your Direct Reports? Would they agree? Any room for improvement?

31
BY DEMONSTRATING
GOOD JUDGMENT

"Experience is simply the name we give our mistakes."
- Oscar Wilde

In your attempt to save time, do you rush and make snap decisions without considering the consequences?

Good judgment is your ability to bring together reason and wisdom to analyze a situation, explore your options, select a course of action, and take action.

Good judgment isn't about being smart or about making good decisions.

The essence of good judgment is about

learning from past mistakes.

It's about using your *Assessment Systems* (Chapter 8) to ensure you don't repeat the same mistakes and increase the probability of success of your next attempt.

Judgment is less about getting it right and more about

what it takes to learn what went wrong.

Some of your decisions will result in *Unintended Consequences*. To add to this uncertainty, you'll soon discover that your decisions aren't always about what's good or bad. Often, they're about choosing between good, better, and best. All decisions have consequences, which you won't see in advance. But experience teaches that they'll come due someday.

Where do good decisions come from?

Good decisions don't happen by accident.

- Good decisions come from good judgment.
- Good judgment comes from failure.
- Failure comes from mistakes.
- Mistakes come from bad decisions.
- Bad decisions come from bad judgment.

- Bad judgment comes from a lack of experience.

- Lack of experience comes from:
  - ✓ Having little time invested in the job.
  - ✓ Not learning from your mistakes.
  - ✓ Not learning from the mistakes of others.
  - ✓ Making quick decisions when you have more time.
  - ✓ A failure to venture outside your comfort zone.

Mistakes, if you learn from them, are the building blocks of greatness.

How can you learn from the mistakes of others?

Learning from the mistakes of others only happens if you're paying attention. The truth is that anyone can cut their learning curve and gain years of valuable experience by using this simple principle:

There are only two ways to learn anything in life, either by trial and error or by modeling the best practices.

While it's important to learn from your mistakes, it's a lot easier to learn from the mistakes of others.

How can Modeling help you?

Experience is the toughest teacher because it gives the test first and the knowledge second. Modeling a better teacher because it gives you the knowledge, so you're better prepared for the test.

Modeling is the process of learning from those who've already achieved success.

It also means learning by copying the behavior of those who've already experienced the mistakes and failures on their journey to success (Chapter 35). You can avoid the same mistakes and failures by learning, applying, and sharing what you'll learn here. Each new skill learned builds on the previous, and the compound effect is career-changing.

32

BY KNOWING WHEN TO
ACT, WAIT OR WALK AWAY

"You got to know when to hold 'em. Know when to fold 'em.
Know when to walk away and know when to run."
- Kenny Rogers, The Gambler.

When faced with a problem, how do you know what to do? For every problem you'll face, you'll normally have three choices of how to respond:

You can act, wait, or walk away.

When faced with a problem, can't you just do nothing? Sure. Think about it. You have this option every time you're faced with a problem. Do some problems sometimes correct themselves by doing nothing? Yes. Do some problems get worse by taking action rather than doing nothing? You bet!

Remember, doing nothing is deciding by default.

Are there some problems that are better left alone? Sure. Just ask any Fire-fighter. Most of the time, all they can do is contain the fire and just let it burn itself out; let it *burn-to-the-ground.* If you feel this is your best choice, among all the choices you have at the time, then do nothing – let it burn-to-the-ground

However, doing nothing and waiting
are two different options.

When faced with any problem, use these steps to guide your response.

Step 1: Should I Act NOW?

Before deciding, answer these questions?

- Can this problem be resolved by calling 911? If Yes, call!

- Will acting now save lives or avoid further damage?

  ✓ If Yes, take *Immediate Action* (Appendix F).

  ✓ If No to both questions, continue to Step 2.

Step 2: Is this my problem?

- Is this my problem or someone else's?

- Who has the most to gain or lose from its resolution?

- Who's affected by this problem?

If this problem isn't your problem, why are you trying to solve it? Just report it to your boss and walk away. If this is your problem, continue to the next step.

Step 3: Should I act now or wait?

- How urgent is this problem?

- How important or urgent is this problem and why?

- What must happen before I'm forced to act?

- What are the consequences if this problem remains unresolved?

- What's the downside of waiting?

- How much time do I have?

- How long do I have before this problem becomes a crisis?

- How long do I have before I'm forced to act?

- When's it too late to act?

Based on your answers to the above questions, use the *Decision Support Template* below to guide your decision.

Here's an example of a *Decision Support Template*: Time vs. Urgency.

Decision Support Matrix		Time to Decide?	
		Little Time	Enough Time
Urgency?	Urgent	1	2
	Not Urgent	3	4

Here's what the numbers mean:

1. If this problem is urgent and you have little time to decide, take *Immediate Action* (Appendix B) and develop a mental *Plan of Action* before acting (Appendix A). See CONPLAN 1.

2. If this problem is urgent and you have enough time, take Step 4. Prepare to act after completing your *Plan of Action*. Keep your boss informed. See CONPLAN 2.

3. If this problem isn't urgent and you have little time to decide, wait, continue to monitor the situation, create your *Plan of Action*, and keep your boss informed. See CONPLAN 3.

4. If this problem isn't urgent and you have enough time to act, continue to monitor the situation, create your *Plan of Action*, and update your boss. See CONPLAN 4.

Also, document what happened, when, and who took what action to resolve the problem for investigative or legal purposes later.

Step 4: Create your Plan of Action.

See Appendix A.

Note: You're responsible for anticipating your work's consequences and effects BEFORE deciding (Chapter 10).

Other Things to Consider

When's the best time to decide?

Do you have to make the decision right now? This classic answer is usually, No! This is rarely necessary. Resist the impulse of making a snap decision when there's no need to do so. Normally, you'll have sufficient time to decide.

> *"The key is not to make quick decisions,*
> *but to make timely decisions."*
> *- Colin Powell*

A good rule of thumb is to decide after acquiring **40-70%** of the information you need. Mistakes, as long as you learn from them, are the building blocks of greatness. If it turns out bad, adjust, and remember what you've learned for next time.

Who's the Best Person to decide?

First, the boss decides! Or, at least, the boss should take responsibility and ownership of his team's decisions, especially if it turns out bad. Ask members for their input before you decide. Also, if the decision affects everyone in your team, why can't all members be given a chance to concur or non-concur with reasons (Chapter 16)?

Does the Best Decision always produce the Best Outcome?

There's a big difference between your decision and the result or outcome of your decision. You could be the most experienced decision-maker on the planet, and you could make the best decision, but there's no guarantee that your problem will be resolved or the best outcome will be achieved. You can make a good decision, and the results could still be bad. The situation and facts available when you first decided could (and probably will) change over time. What was good today could turn out to be bad tomorrow.

Do you need your Boss's Approval?

Have you ever been in a situation where you were waiting for your boss's approval? Why are you asking for approval if the problem is internal, doesn't require additional resources you don't have, and isn't in conflict with any internal standards? Of course, that's what your boss is paying you to do. But do let him know.

Sometimes it's easier to ask forgiveness than permission.

Or, if you're in doubt, tell your boss when you'll be making your decision (like the end of the week), and if you don't hear from him before that time, you'll be moving forward. Don't forget to assess the consequences and effects of your actions.

What if a Direct Reports recommends a change?

One of the best bosses I ever worked with once said,

> *"If I can't give you a good reason not to make the change; I'll approve it."*

Yes, they still had to create a *Decision Paper* (Appendix B), build consensus with the team (Chapter 16), and present it to the team for a final discussion before approval. However, this gave the team the freedom they needed to make things better.

33

BY FOLLOWING UP
AND FOLLOWING-THROUGH

"Learning the secrets and skill of great No.2s remains
the surest path to becoming No. 1."
- David Heenan and Warren Bennis.

Do you know how to *Follow up* and *Follow-through* to increase your probability of success and enhance your effectiveness and credibility at work?

By Following up

Many mistakes and failures in business can be traced back to someone who failed to *Follow up*.

Follow up is a subsequent action taken to check on the validity of an initial action.

And there are three situations where *Follow up* is needed.

Situation 1.
When someone fails to respond to your solicitation.

Using a sales example, if a prospect fails to respond to your solicitation or declines to do business with you, you still should *Follow up. Follow-up* means continuing to contact them until you receive a positive response. The secret is to continue to add value to the person you're trying to reach.

Situation 2.
When you're trying to contact someone to resolve a problem.

Here are the most important steps if you're trying to resolve a problem (like poor customer service, a faulty product, or a delayed order).

Step 1. Call to resolve the problem.

Record the date, whom you spoke with, and their response.

Step 2. Leave a detailed voicemail message.

If you get their voicemail, always leave a message giving the date, your name, company, phone number, a detailed description of the problem with its reference number, and a request for a return call.

Step 3. Document your actions.

Always document your *follow-up* action. This way, when your boss asks, you can show him your *"Action Log."*

Step 4. Show up in person.

After you've called three times with no response, show up in person and get your problem resolved.

Step 5. Add it to your Unresolved Issues List.

Until resolved, keep this issue on your *Unresolved Issues List* and ensure your boss has a current copy (Chapter 9).

Situation 3.
After delegating an assignment or making a reservation or appointment.

Follow up also means contacting someone a few days before the due date of your assignment, reservation or appointment to confirm it's still valid.

Delegating an assignment isn't abdication because the asker is still responsible and accountable for the end-result.

5% of delegating is asking someone to perform a task by a certain time. The other 95% is about following up to ensure it gets done.

A good 30% of the time, my reservations or appointments got lost. I assumed that all was good-to-go, and I was sadly mistaken.

Here's a great story of how it should be done

On June 1st, Joe was asked by his boss to set up a luncheon for 30 senior executives at the best steak house in town for June 15th. This was two weeks before the luncheon when Joe made the initial reservation. He recorded the date, time, and the name of the person he spoke with on his Assignment Tracking Form (Appendix F).

On June 12th, a few days before the luncheon, as Joe was reviewing his Assignment Tracking Form, he decided to follow up, and here's how it went.

Hi, this is Joe Sanchez from Trident Resources. I'm calling to follow up on the reservation for our company's luncheon for Thursday, June 15th, at 11:30 AM? Is everything still on track?

The scheduler said, "Joe, I don't have a reservation for your company. When did you make it and whom did you speak with? After looking at his Assignment Tracking Form, Joe said, "I called two weeks ago, on June 1st, and I spoke to Carol Brown."

After a long pause, the scheduler continued, "Carol was let go two weeks ago. That may explain the problem. Then, after another long pause, she said, "Joe, you're lucky. You called just in time. If you had waited another day, you'd be out of luck." After Joe's heart rate returned to normal, he was glad he documented all his phone calls and followed up when he did. If not, he would have had 30 senior executives standing around looking for a place to eat. Not good.

By Following-through

This is what your boss means when he says, *"Get back to me, let me know, or keep me in the loop."*

Follow-through is the process of returning to the asker, either face-to-face or on the phone, and reporting the status of their request.

There are two situations where *Follow-through* is needed.

Situation 1.
When your boss or customer asks you to do something.

When this happens, make sure you have a clear understanding of what the boss or customer wants to be done (the task) and when he needs it completed (the deadline). If you have any questions, ask! If you can't deliver, speak up! After completing the task, *Return and Report*, either face-to-face or on the phone.

Return and Report mean contacting the asker, either face-to-face or on the phone, to update the status of their request.

If you can't complete the task as requested, return, either face-to-face or on the phone, and report the problem. Also, recommend what should be done to resolve the problem.

Returning and Reporting is the most important part of Following-through.

Situation 2.
When you ask a Direct Report to do something.

When you ask a Direct Report to do something, ensure you tell him WHAT you want to be done (the task) and WHEN you need it completed (the deadline).

Also, ask him to *Follow-through*. You may have to explain what you mean. Explain that you want him to *Return and Report*, either face-to-face or on the phone when the task is completed. If he can't complete the task, ask him to return, either face-to-face or on the phone, and report the problem and recommend what needs to be done to resolve it.

The most effective people I know, those at the top of their game, do something special.

They over-communicate!

They Follow-through even if they have nothing new.

This way, I know I wasn't forgotten!

When you *Follow-through*, you'll stand out above the rest.

Note: When you tell someone that *"I'm-on-it,"* you've just said to them that you'd *Follow-through*.

34
BY ASSESSING PERFORMANCE

"Followership, like leadership, is a role and not a destination."
- Michael McKinney

Do you know how to measure the performance of members, teams, and systems to enhance their ability to consistently produce excellent results? Are they getting better or worse? How do you know for sure? Your performance includes your results, behavior, and potential.

Effective people don't just set the bar; they are the bar.

What's the best way to measure performance?

The best way to measure performance is by using solid, objective measurements. Actual performance measurement is a more effective way to evaluate results because the measurement is relevant to the situation or process. Some of the best ways to assess performance are by using *Metrics, Objectives and Key Results (OKRs), Key Performance Indicators (KPIs), and Bands of Excellence (BOEs).*

By using Metrics

Metrics are quantifiable and allow you to set the <u>desired</u> result compared to the <u>actual</u> result, but there's a downside.

A metric is something used to measure and track the results of members, teams, or systems to assess its performance.

Here's a Good Story:

Bob was assigned to improve the number of "problem fixes per day" called into the Helpdesk in his company. He spent a few hours in the Helpdesk Call Center to observe. To his amazement, he found that each Helpdesk Operator was assessed daily using 17 different metrics. One metric was how much "time the operator spent on the phone." The operators were told to keep each call to less than two minutes, which was counterproductive in solving the caller's problems. After a few hours, Bob determined that working under these conditions (metrics) was not where he wanted to work.

His intuition told him that the metrics were too restrictive. He directed that all metrics be stopped except for one; the number of "problems fixed per day."

Result? The number of *"problems fixed per day"* shot up off the charts. Problem solved! So, be careful with all your metrics. Sometimes less is more. Focus on the most important metrics – the ones that make sense.

Here are some typical metrics:

Cash Flow: Cash flow is the money coming in and out of your business on any given day, which is what you use to cover your business expenses, such as payroll, rent, and inventory.

Customer: Customer Acquisition Cost (CAC). Divide your total acquisition costs by the number of new customers over the same time frame you're examining.

Employee: Employee Turnover Rate (ETR). To determine your ETR, take the number of employees who have departed the company and divide it by the average number of employees. If you have a high ETR, spend some time examining your workplace culture, employment packages, and work environment.

By using Objectives and Key Results (OKRs)

An OKR (or Objectives and Key Results) is a framework for defining and tracking objectives and their outcomes.

OKR is generally attributed to **Andy Grove**, CEO of Intel, who introduced the approach to Intel during his tenure there and documented this in his 1983 book *High Output Management*. OKRs comprise an Objective, a clearly defined goal, and one or more Key Results (specific measures used to track the achievement of that objective).

OKRs:

- May be shared across the company to provide teams with visibility of goals to align and focus effort.

- Are typically set at the company, team, and personal levels, although there's criticism that this causes too much of a *waterfall approach*, where OKRs are trying to be just the opposite.

- Overlap with other performance management frameworks - complexity sitting somewhere between KPI and the balanced scorecard.

The idea took hold, and OKRs quickly became central to Google's culture as a "management methodology" that helps ensure that the company focuses effort on the same important issues. Since becoming popular at Google, OKR has favored several similar tech start-ups, including LinkedIn, Twitter, and Uber. For more on OKRs, review the book or audiobook, *Measure What Matters* by **John Doerr.**

By using Key Performance Indicators (KPI)

KPIs provide a company with a focus for strategic and operational improvement and compare achievements to similar companies.

A Key Performance Indicator (KPI) is a performance measure that demonstrates how effectively a company is at achieving its key objectives.

To be effective, a *KPI* must be well-defined and quantifiable, communicated throughout your company, crucial to achieving the goal, and applicable to the business.

What's the difference between a Metric and a KPI?

KPIs support business goals and objectives.

Metrics support *KPIs* and focus on the overall tactical business goals and objectives.

Meaningful performance measures start with measurable goals. This means that your goal needs to be clear enough that you can imagine how you'll recognize it when it becomes real. So, you might first want to check if your current goals are measurable. Members won't *buy-in* to something they don't understand, weren't involved with, and see no relevance.

The key to deriving *KPIs* from objectives is to work backward and reverse engineer the *metrics* you want to create. This process is called goal, question, metric. Your objectives are your goals for your business or project.

By using Bands of Excellence (BOE)

Since *Public-Sector Organizations,* like teachers or government workers, don't focus on profit generation, what matters most to their survival is providing a service that serves the greater good (like schools and government agencies). But how do they do that? They use a metric called a *Band of Excellence (or BOE)* to measure and assess their level of services.

Those who work in the Public-Sector must maintain their *Band of Excellence (BOE)* set by their organization.

Think of *BOEs* as the desired Standard of Performance for members, units, and systems.

A Band of Excellence is a set of performance limits ranging from the Minimum (or Standard) performance limit to the Maximum performance limit.

The difference between the minimum and the maximum is called the *Band of Excellence.* If your performance stays within the *Band of Excellence,* you remain employable.

Here's a simple example:

The biggest government agency on the planet is the US Department of Defense. In 1992, as a former US Army Officer, here's the BOE used to measure physical fitness by taking the Annual Physical Fitness Test.

The BOE Minimum (or Standard) was 200 points overall. The BOE Maximum was 300 points overall. Therefore, the BOE was 200 - 300 for the test overall to remain promotable.

If a Soldier failed to achieve 200 points overall, he was retrained and retested. If he failed a second time, he was considered un-promotable and administratively processed for release from the military.

By Tracking Trends

Have you ever tried to measure how you and your unit were doing? If not, you will. In every viable business, key metrics help determine the answer to one simple question: Are we getting better *Over-Time*?

Over-time means as compared to a past time (last month or year).

And ask the same question about yourself, *are you getting better over-time?* And your business unit, *is my business unit getting better over-time?* But how can you tell?

Here's a good example:

Think of *KPIs* as your Doctor does when you go for a physical.

Step 1: What gets measured? They measure the most important aspects of optimum health, like weight, height, blood pressure, pulse, temperature, and cholesterol.

Step 2: If this is your first physical, how do your numbers compare to a healthy person your age (what's the norm, standard, or benchmark)? Any corrective action needed?

Step 3: If this isn't your first physical, how do your numbers compare to your last physical? Are you (your physical system) getting better *over-time*? Any corrective action needed?

Use this same process with all your *Key Performance Indicators*. What are the things you can measure that tell you about the health of your unit?

Are you getting better over-time?

If not, why? What can be done (corrective action) to reverse the numbers? What number is acceptable to you? What are your standards? If this number rises above or falls below a certain level, what corrective action must be taken? One way to visually track your *KPIs* is to measure and compare your numbers *over-time*, the trend. What does the trend look like? Is it trending in the right direction? By doing so, you'll be able to see if the trend is getting better or worse.

Here's an example of Tracking Trends.

Accounts Receivable, 90-Days Past Due (As of June 21, 20XX)			
This month	**Last month**	**2-Months ago**	**1-Year Ago**
$15,335	$12,457	$10,237	$25,936

Notice that this table is tracking a *Key Performance Indicator* that measures *Accounts Receivable over 90 days*. Therefore, the status ("This Month") is greater than last and the month before. In other words, your *90-Day Past Due* numbers are increasing or getting worse.

Tip: Check your unit's usage rate or consumption rate metrics over-time and see what you learn.

35

BY LEARNING FROM
MISTAKES AND FAILURE

"If you're not making mistakes, then you're not doing anything.
I'm positive that a doer makes mistakes."
- John Wooden

Will you make mistakes and have failures in your lifetime? You bet lots of them. But that's how we all learn. So, how can you learn from mistakes and failure? Effective people know that the only thing that matters is what you learn for the next time regarding mistakes and failure.

What's Failure?

The dictionary defines failure as:

"The state or condition of not meeting a desirable or intended goal and may be viewed as the opposite of success."

Failure is a relative term. It's viewed differently depending on your situation and who's doing the viewing. For example, failure to a baseball player may be striking out, but failure to his coach might be losing the game.

In the Business World, your goals will come from your boss. Did you accomplish the goals you were assigned? Did you achieve the result you wanted? If not, why?

The only important question is, what did you learn that can make you better next time? I used to think that there was no such thing as failure (it didn't exist) as long as you never gave up. But this is only partially true and sends the wrong message. Of course, you'll experience mistakes and failures in your life. The trick is not to let them define you.

Instead, let them Refine you and make you stronger!

The past doesn't equal the future. So, learn what you need to learn and move on!

What's the difference between a failure and an unsuccessful attempt?

- **Failure** needs a substantial loss (like money, time, or reputation).

- An **Unsuccessful Attempt** means that your last attempt did not achieve the desired result.

However, if you can make another attempt, did you learn why the last attempt was unsuccessful? Do you know what changes need to be made for your next attempt to be successful?

The example most often used comes from the story of *Thomas Edison* and his 10,000 attempts to create the incandescent light bulb. Just remember, *Edison* could make as many attempts as he needed until he was successful because he wasn't paying for each attempt. His investors were paying the bills. Most people don't have that luxury.

Failure only exists if there's a loss.

The bigger the loss, the bigger the failure.

What's Failure in the Real World?

There are two types of failure which are commonly misunderstood:

- **Personal failure:** This is an unsuccessful attempt at accomplishing your personal goal and includes a:

  - ✓ **Failure to try.** This is never setting goals or never attempting to accomplish anything.

  - ✓ **Failure to keep trying.** This means that after an unsuccessful initial attempt, you failed to learn from your mistakes, make the changes needed, find a different way to get there, or make another attempt.

  - ✓ **Substantial Loss.** This is a loss of your wealth, relationships, health, *character, or reputation.

- **Company failure:** This is a failure to accomplish an assigned goal, resulting in losing anything your boss couldn't afford to lose.

*To learn more about **Character**, available at **Amazon.com,** see page 5.

Let's examine what should happen BEFORE you attempt to accomplish any goal.

Before the Attempt

Step 1. What's the Risk?

Conduct a *Risk Assessment* to look for all the things that could reasonably go wrong during your attempt. Then, collaborate to assess all your safety, security, financial, and operational risk and how they can be mitigated.

Step 2. How many attempts?

If you know you'll only get one attempt, make it count! If you know you'll get more than one attempt, but not an unlimited number, then you have some risk, but how can this be mitigated? On the other hand, if you know you'll get as many attempts as you need, then the only risk is the cost of each additional attempt. Remember *Edison*?

Step 3. What's the cost?

Cost: What will it cost to make this attempt (how much time, money, or effort will it take)?

Opportunity Costs: What are you losing by not using other alternatives?

Step 4. What if you're wrong?

Can everyone live with an unsuccessful attempt?

Step 5. What are the benefits?

What benefits will you receive if your attempt is successful?

Step 6. Is the benefit worth the cost?

If Yes: Continue to create your *Plan of Action* (Appendix A).

If No or Unsure: Work hard to mitigate your Risk. Then, conduct another Cost/Benefit Analysis.

Step 7. What's your Assessment System?

An *Assessment System* is a series of procedures designed to measure the most critical parameters of your attempt to determine what went wrong, right, and why (Chapter 8)? How will the attempt be measured? How do you know when it's time to *pull-the-plug?*

After the Attempt

Let's examine what should happen AFTER your attempt.

Step 8. Was the attempt a complete success?

If Yes: Congrats! What's next?

If No: If your attempt was unsuccessful, was there a loss?

If there was **NO loss**, what did you learn, and what changes need to be made? Never give up! Just find another way to get there.

If there was a loss, now you have a real failure. The greater the loss, the greater the failure.

Step 9. What did you learn from your Assessment System?

- What went wrong, right, and why?

- What needs to change to make your next attempt a success?

- How will you know when it's time to *pull-the-plug*?

The lesson may have been painful, but don't throw the learning away. Mistakes and failures can be your best teacher, but only if you remember the lesson. Now what? Well, that depends on you!

Is Failure Fatal?

"Failure is not fatal, but failure to change might be."
– John Wooden

Assuming your attempt resulted in a loss, it's not the end of your life or your career. And, sometimes, getting close is good enough. So, assess what happened, what you learned, and get *back-in-the-game!*

Never give up! Just find another way to get there.

Can you achieve Success without Failure?

"If things are not failing, you are not innovating enough."
- Elon Musk

For all of **Elon Musk's** success, he has experienced an equal amount of failure. Whatever future success he achieves will most likely be accompanied by more failure.

Here are three times Elon Musk failed:

1. Once, he couldn't get a CEO job to save his life.

When Zip2 began attracting investors, they stripped him of his role as Chairman. Musk's idea of leadership in the 1990s was to stay late and rewrite code, believing his employees were incompetent. He failed to see how publicly berating his employees might make them less productive.

2. He has crashed more than his share of rockets.

His career serves as ample proof that the first step to success is a whole bunch of failures. Until April 8, 2016, the company managed the first of three consecutive successful landings. The results in June resulted in four rocket launches in a row ending in flames.

3. He has never delivered a car on time.

Tesla revealed that it built only 260 Model 3 vehicles, instead of the promised 1,500, with no chance of making the originally claimed 5,000 by the end of the year. Shipments were initially expected to begin in 2013, yet the first cars didn't ship until late 2015.

By comparison, it took Amazon more than 14 years to make as much profit as it produced the previous quarter. Amazon consistently lost money for its first several years as a public company.

Lessons Learned: Constantly seek criticism and feedback; it's as good as gold! Never give up. Just find another way to get there.

"Being an entrepreneur starting up is like eating glass and staring into the abyss of death."
- Unknown

This page is intentionally left blank.

APPENDIX A:
PLAN OF ACTION EXAMPLE

Do you know how to create a *Project Plan of Action* to move your work forward? Here's a real-world example of a *Plan of Action*.

Situation: Using *Role-Playing*, let's assume your name is Bob, and it's May 1, 20XX. You've just been told by your boss (the Director of IT) that you're the Project Manager for the Company Picnic on June 21st.

This means that you're *in-charge*, so *take-charge* by completing your draft POA. You visited the picnic site, and you've spoken to last year's Project Manager and learned that it rained last year, and everyone was soaked. From last year's survey results, you learned that the only condiment was ketchup.

You're the Manager of IT within your company. You have five Direct Reports. Each Direct Report has five entry-level team members that report to them.

You decide that there are five main tasks to be performed to make the picnic a success:

- Prepare and serve picnic food and drink.
- Provide entertainment.
- Present awards.
- Conduct youth activities.
- Conduct picnic clean-up.

But who should be assigned to perform these tasks?

During your *Backbriefing,* you present these options to your boss:

Option 1: You could contract out some of the work. However, your boss has already told you that this will be done internally.

Option 2: You could perform all major tasks yourself. You quickly realize that the sheer scope of the assignment would cause you to be overwhelmed.

Option 3: You could share the load by assigning one major task to each of the other major units within the company. Your boss disagrees and reminds you that you don't have assignment authority outside your IT Unit. But nice try!

Option 4: You could assign these five tasks to your five Direct Reports. You decide to take this option because you and your boss agree that this is the best of the four options available.

DRAFT PLAN OF ACTION (POA) FOR A COMPANY PICNIC

Subject: Draft *Plan of Action* for Company Picnic, June 21, 20XX

Objective: ABC Company (Who) conducts their annual picnic (What) on June 21, 20XX, from 12:00 to 4:30 PM (When), at Mason Park, Lot 14, (Where) to improve morale, have fun, get to know each other, and celebrate our accomplishments (Why - Purpose). If it rain, the picnic will move to the Jefferson High School Gymnasium.

Methods: (How)

Concept: ABC Picnic will be conducted in three phases:

- **Phase 1:** Set-up of food, entertainment, and activities begin at 10 AM at Mason Park.

- **Phase 2:** The picnic will begin at 12:00 and end at 4:30 PM.

- **Phase 3:** Clean-up will begin at 4:30 PM until finished.

Specific Instructions:

Key Players	Major Tasks	Jun 21@	Notes
Bill	Set up and run youth activities	NLT 12:00	See Youth Activities enclosure
John	Clean-up picnic site	4:30 PM	Bring trash bags
Lisa	Provide musical entertainment	12:00 to 4:30 PM	See Entertainment enclosure
Joe	Prepare and serve picnic meal.	Serve NLT 12:00	See Picnic Menu enclosure. Ensure plenty of condiments!
Mary Anne	Prepare/present awards	Present at 1 PM	See Awards enclosure. Rehearsal on June 20, 1 PM in our conference room

General Instructions: Dress is casual. Bring plenty of sunscreen and blankets or folding chairs to sit on.

Risk:

- Safety: Bring plenty of Sunscreen.
- Security: Lock your car and do not leave valuables in your car.
- Financial: N/A
- Assumptions: Headcount will be the same as last year (150 people).

Timetable: See enclosure 2 (Timetable)

Resources Needed:

Who (Unit)	What	Where	Jun 21 @
Joe	4-Folding tables for food, 3-Grills	Lot 14, Mason Park	NLT 11:30
Mary Anne	Public Address system	Lot 14, Mason Park	NLT 11:30
Bill	Youth Game Equipment	Lot 14, Mason Park	NLT 11:30

Unresolved Issues: See enclosure 1 (*Unresolved Issues List*)

FOR THE DIRECTOR:

Your Signature:

Project Manager: Bob Murray, email, and phone number.

Distribution: 1-Each Key Player, 1-Your Boss, 1-File

Enclosures:

1: *Unresolved Issues List (Enclosure 1)*

2: *Timetable (Enclosure 2)*

3: Program Schedule (To Be Published)

4: Changes (TBP)

5: Youth Activities (TBP)

6: Picnic Menu (TBP)

7: Awards (TBP)

Enclosure 1: *Unresolved Issues List*

Unresolved Issue List					
Date	Unresolved Issue	Assigned	Deadline	Checked	Status
~~May 4~~	~~Which youth games?~~	~~Bill~~	~~May 6~~		~~Answered~~
May 5	No money is available	Joe	May 7		On-going

Don't delete anything from this list. You'll need them later. Just ~~Strike Through~~ them when they are both <u>known</u> and <u>acceptable to you</u>.

Enclosure 2: *Timetable*:

Partial Timetable for Company Picnic (June 21)							
Yr	M	D	Time	Preventive Actions	Responsible	Where	Who
14	5	2	1 PM	Site visit conducted	Bob	B	
14	5	4	2 PM	Backbriefing	Bob	A	
14	5	4		Advanced Warning	Bob		
14	5	6		Draft POA Staffed	Bob		
14	5	10		Final Decision Briefing	Bob	A	2
14	5	12		Final POA distributed	Bob		
14	5	25	2 PM	IPR #1: Milestone 1	All	A	2
14	6	1		Promotion begins	Bob		
14	6	1		Request resources	Joe		
14	6	14	2 PM	IPR #2: Milestone 2	All	A	2
14	6	19	1 PM	Final site visit	Bob	B	2
14	6	20		Buy Food & Drinks	Joe		
14	6	20	1 PM	Rehearsals	Bob	A	2
14	6	21	10 AM	Equipment set-up	Joe	B	2
14	6	21	12:00	Company Picnic	All	B	1
14	6	22	12:0	After-Action Review	All	B	1

B
CREATE A
DECISION PAPER

Do you know how to create a convincing *Decision Paper* or a *Business Case* to persuade someone to spend the money needed to move your work forward? Have you ever been asked to write a *Decision Paper or a Business Case*? If not, you will. This is one way your boss is preparing you for the next level.

Sometimes you'll need resources that you don't have, like people, equipment, or facilities, to solve a problem – which means spending money. When this happens, you'll need the DM's approval before moving forward. To persuade anyone to accept your recommendation, you'll need a well-written *Decision Paper,* and here's a great format.

What's the best format for a Decision Paper?

1. Subject. Briefly state the subject.

2. Problem. State the problem in one sentence.

3. Recommendation. State the recommended solution in one sentence.

4. Benefits: State the expected benefits of this recommendation.

5. Key Player Comments.

A Key Player is anyone whose opinion would matter to the Decision-Maker or anyone who'll be required to support the recommendation if approved. You'll need to *Staff* your paper through all Key Players for their concurrence or non-concurrence with comments (Chapter 16). Once comments are returned, create a table showing which Key Players concurred or non-concurred with their reasons.

6. Discussion. Explain why you're recommending this solution by answering these questions.

- **What were all the solutions you considered?** Then, attach all the solutions you considered with all the Advantages and Disadvantages.

- **Why did you select this solution?**

- **What's the cost and who should pay?**

- **What's the Risk?** How probable is this risk, how severe will it be, and how can it be mitigated (Chapters 17-19). If a *Contingency Plan* is needed, add it as an enclosure (Chapter 21).

- **How long will it take, and when should it be started?**

- **How long do we have before this problem becomes a crisis?**

- **What are the consequences and effects?** *Unintended Consequences* are outcomes that are not expected from your project. *2nd and 3rd Order Effects* deal with how your project affects others, like those in your company or your suppliers (Chapter 10).

- **What are the *Unresolved Issues*?** Attach a list of all the questions, unknowns, concerns, shortfalls, obstacles, and problems that could slow or stop your progress (Chapter 9).

- **What are all the Facts and Assumptions?** Attach a list of all the facts and assumptions you used (Appendix C).

When your paper is finished, give a Decision Briefing or provide a hard copy to the DM to gain approval. If you choose this option, ensure your paper is no more than two pages in length, with all the supporting documents attached as enclosures.

What's a Business Case?

A *Decision Paper* is also known as a *Business Case*, which is the justification to convince a Decision-Maker to accept a proposal.

A Business Case is a document that captures the reasons for initiating action.

The logic is that whenever resources are consumed, they should support a specific business need. For example, it could be a software upgrade needed to improve system performance. The *Business Case* is that a software upgrade would improve customer satisfaction, require less processing time, or reduce maintenance costs. Thus, a compelling *Business Case* captures both the quantifiable and non-quantifiable characteristics of the proposed action.

C
GATHER
ASSUMPTIONS AND FACTS

Do you know how to gather all the assumptions, facts, and the truth needed to persuade others to support you to enhance your probability of success?

By identifying the Assumptions

An ASSUMPTION is information accepted as true in the absence of facts.

However, acceptable assumptions must pass two tests.

- They must be **VALID**, which means that they're likely to be true.

- They must be **NECESSARY**, which means that they're essential to moving the work forward.

If the process can continue without the assumption, discard it. If the assumption is both valid and necessary, then treat it as a fact. Effective people continually seek to confirm their assumptions by testing.

If you assume that the weather won't be a problem for your company's outdoor picnic, you better have a *Contingency Plan* - just in case. Better yet, if it rains and you've reserved an outdoor picnic site with overhead cover, now you're the hero of the day.

You know the old saying about assumptions, right?

Whenever you assume anything, you risk making an 'ass' out of 'u' and 'me.'

So, be careful! People aren't mind readers. Never assume everyone understands your expectations. It doesn't matter how much experience you have or how long you've been in your position. If you feel there's a chance of a misunderstanding, clarify all your expectations by asking better questions.

Here's an example:

"As an executive coach, one of my C-level clients shared with me his disappointment with a new VP he recently hired. He explained that he told his new VP that he expected him to really "step up" and get us to "the next level" in sales.

However, after six months, he and his sales team had not met his expectations. I asked him, "Have you defined what 'stepping up' and 'getting to the next level' mean?" My client responded, "No, why would I? With his experience, he should know what I mean." Ops!

What's an Unconscious Assumption?

Sometimes assumptions are made unconsciously. So, be careful!

Here's a great example:

Bob walked into a Problem-Solving Session where one of his Direct Reports, with his entire team, tried to select the BEST vendor from two similar companies. As the process was almost over, Bob asked, "What assumptions are you making here?" Then, after a long silence, he asked the question again.

One person said, "None, we don't need any." To which Bob said, "Are you sure? Since I only see two vendors you're considering, aren't you assuming that there are only two companies that we could potentially hire to solve this problem? Are you all certain this assumption is correct?

And, what's the effect if later this assumption proves to be incorrect? What happens later when we find out that there was a third company that could have solved our problem faster and at half the cost?" Again, there was a long silence. The group had assumed there were only two potential companies, and they were wrong.

What assumptions are you making unconsciously, and what are the effects on the project if these assumptions turn out to be wrong? What's your *Contingency Plan*?

How can you identify your Assumptions?

To help identify your assumptions, answer these questions:

- What do I hope is true or necessary for my document to be valid?
- What assumptions are needed to move the work forward?
- What assumptions am I making unconsciously?
- If my assumption becomes false, what's my *Contingency Plan* (Chapter 21)?

Always Test your Assumptions and Vet your Facts!

By identifying the Facts

A FACT is verifiable or vetted information.

Always separate facts from opinion or speculation. According to **Colin Powell,** in his book*, It Worked for Me*, you need good information to make good decisions. Verifiable information can change over time and may not tell the whole story. So, be careful! Also, verifiable or vetted facts that come with these qualifiers should make you nervous:

> *"In my best judgment," or "As far as I know" or "As best as I can tell."*

Here are the most important questions you need to answer:

> *What do you know? How do you know for sure?*
> *What do you need to know?*

> *What do you think? What's your best hunch?*
> *What's your intuition telling you?*

Always distinguish the difference. You're looking for *ground-truth*, first-hand info from people closest to the issue. The best facts are current, from a reliable source, and first-hand information rather than hearsay.

By uncovering the Truth

In solving any problem, you must uncover the root cause - the truth. The dictionary defines truth as *"that which is true or in accordance with fact or reality."*

Because of this, most people believe that all facts are true, but they're not. They're related but different.

> *Facts can lead you to the truth,*
>
> *but they can also mislead you.*

Facts are what happened, while the truth is HOW and WHY it happened.

And here are a few examples.

Fact: Mary was my best student. But the truth is that Mary was my only student.

Fact: Sam sold nothing in May. However, the truth is that Sam was on vacation in May.

Facts without context can be misleading, and like statistics, they can be manipulated to prove or disprove just about anything. Facts can't speak for themselves. Someone else must speak for them.

Remember, nothing has meaning other than the meaning you give it. So, be careful!

What's Objective Truth?

"One of the greatest challenges in this world is to know enough about a subject to think your right, but not enough about the subject to know your wrong."

I learned from **Neal deGrasse Tyson's** *Master Class* the three categories of truth: personal, political, and objective. Objective truth is truth no matter what happens and is the truth that shapes our understanding of the universe.

"We all have susceptibility to bias. The internet is evidence of bias. And you're going to use it as evidence that you're correct? No!!!"

D
"DON'T
FORGIT NOTHIN"

Do you know how to prepare for your next project to ensure you haven't forgotten anything? Here are the most important things to consider:

Communications: Do you have direct communication with your Key Players via cell phone or 2-way radios with backup batteries and chargers? Does everyone have a list of each other's phone numbers? What if they're not near their cell phone when you call (or are on another call)?

Fun: Laughter, humor, music, breaks, snacks, games, awards, recognition, surprises, and prizes.

Getting attendees involved: How can you put attendees to work? Have them physically do simulations, problem-solving, breakout sessions, circuit training, seminars, workshops, round-robin stations, role-playing, practical exercises, competition, or small group discussions.

Headquarters: Is there a known location at the event or activity, with a dedicated phone number that's open 24/7 that tracks attendance, safety, and first aid. Do they have a vehicle, driver, and map to the nearest hospital?

Life Support: How will the participants be physically sustained (includes food, drink, snacks, ice, communications, lodging (if overnight), transportation, hygiene, toilets, electricity, cooking, refrigeration, liability insurance, sanitation (hand sanitizer, toilet paper), overhead shelter (if it rains), trash containers, and trash collection and removal). The longer the time and distance from home base, the more complicated the life support becomes.

Other: Parking, access for delivery vehicles, traffic flow, who tracks who's there and who's not? Do you have a backup location in case of bad weather? Did you delegate all these tasks? Do you have consensus from all Key Players?

Pre-work: Do you want the participants to do something before the event and bring it with them? Do they need to review a read-ahead packet? If so, provide it in advance.

Program Support: Audio and visual aids, handouts, loud-speaker, music, surveys, or backup generators?

Promotion: How can you best advertise the event or activity that creates interest and anticipation? What's in it for them? What would make members want to attend? How will you communicate this to all invitees?

Quality Control (Assessment): IPRs, AARs, meetings, deliverables, accountability, surveys, Contingency, Mitigation Plans, Project Updates, metrics, milestones, Timetables, and achieving consensus?

Rehearsals: What do you need to see before you start? Do you need to practice, preview, or rehearse anything before the event or activity? Who's reviewing documents to see if they make sense and are correct?

Safety and Medical: What if someone gets hurt? Do you need first aid kits, defibrillators, life jackets (if around water), and fire extinguishers? Are there any other hazards (like holes, cliffs, water, or any way anyone could get hurt)? How can you mitigate this risk? Do you need members trained in CPR and first aid? How about Bee stings (EpiPen® need a prescription), bug spray, location of the nearest hospital, vehicle designated to transport, maps to hospital, cell phones with 911 capabilities, and an ambulance needed on the site?

Schedule or Program: Is there ample time built into the program for all to have fun and do something meaningful instead of just sitting there? How about a mixer (with name tags) so members can get to meet and know each other?

Search Plan: What happens when someone is reported "missing," especially if away from the company's property?

Security: Are chaperones, guards, police, crowd and traffic control, or checkers needed? Cell phones (with chargers/extra batteries), cameras, and phone# available? Are metal detectors needed to check for weapons?

Site Transition: Site problems also include the poor scheduling of other units before and after your scheduled time. The concern here is that the previous unit may not be cleared of the site before you try to set-up. And this includes your departure at the end of your project before the next unit attempts to move in. Additionally, many units try to pre-stage and move supplies and equipment the night before the project. Ensure you know who'll be there before you and who is coming in after you to ensure the handoff is smooth.

Small Children: Children are a unique challenge because they're so mobile and seem to find their way, unsupervised, into places where they could potentially get hurt. If there's water, you'll need life vests, lifeguards, and the like. If there's a fire or anything hot, or vehicle traffic, wells, or cliffs - get the idea?

Time: What are the start and end times? What else is going on around the selected site during this time? What else is going on in the lives of those assigned to perform certain activities like graduations, summer vacations, or the Super Bowl? Hint? What happened last year at the same time and place? What's your *Contingency Plan*?

Note: You may not need all these reminders for your next project, but it's an excellent checklist to add to your toolbox.

What are you forgetting to do?

This page is intentionally left blank.

E

TRACK
ALL THE MOVING PARTS

Do you know how to keep track of all your moving parts to ensure that nothing *falls-through-the-cracks* to enhance your probability of success?

"Tracking" means keeping a paper or digital trail (documenting) of the most important things that keep changing.

How do you keep track of all the things that are critical to your work? Effective people know that there are many " moving parts " in business, and many lose their way - unless someone tracks them.

Here are several ways to keep track of your most important "moving parts."

By Tracking Assignments

Assignments come in two types; Assignments *Accepted* from others and Assignments *Made* to others.

Here's an example of an *Assignments Tracking Form.*

Assignments Accepted					Assignments Made			
Date	From	Action Item	DL	To	Date	DL	Checked	Status
11 May	Boss	ABC Report	19 Jun	Sue	12 May	17 Jun	2 Jun	OS

Notice that this table tracks the assignments *accepted* from others (boss) and the assignments *made* to others. It's also a good idea to assign the *Action Item* to a Direct Report (Sue), with her deadline (DL) being a few days before your boss's deadline. This way, you have some *slack time* built in just in case something goes wrong.

For example, using this table, if your boss wants his assignment completed on May 19th, assign your Direct Report (Sue) a deadline of May 17th. This is your record of all assignments *made* for future meetings.

You can also create an *Assignment Tracking Form* for each Direct Report to use during your internal meetings. The most important thing to remember is to never trust your memory. Always document everything you've asked a Direct Report to do and add a deadline.

By Tracking Changes

Have you ever been frustrated with last-minute changes to a project? Have you ever tried to communicate a change to all Key Players, but 10% didn't get the word? Plans change, so be flexible! Make sure all Key Players know about all changes. Keep a record of who was told what, when, and how. It will come in handy later. Keep track of everyone who received the changes. Record and review these changes during your meetings.

Here's an example of a *Change Notification List.*

Change List for: _____ Project (As of Aug 21, 20XX)				
Date	What Changed?	Originator?	Recipient?	How sent?
May 4	Add 12 to headcount	Bill	John	Phone
May 5	Next meeting 10 AM, not 9 AM.	Joe	Sam	Face-to-face

Notice that this table tracks the *Originator* or the source of the change, the *Recipient* or who was told about the change, and the *How Sent* or how the message was communicated.

If it's important or time-sensitive, don't use email. Many people fail to read their email for days, if at all. Many others misunderstand their email. The best means of communicating is *face-to-face* (second is on the phone). Then, *follow-through* with a detailed email. Don't use email as your primary means of communication. Who else needs to know this info? Act on that answer!

By Tracking Unresolved Issues

Track all *Unresolved Issues,* including any question, unknown, concern, shortfall, obstacle, or problem that could slow or stop your progress (Chapter 9). Each issue can only be eliminated when it's both *"known for certain"* and *"acceptable to you."* If you fail to keep track of all the moving parts, expect that you'll be known as someone who doesn't have their act together.

F
TAKE
IMMEDIATE ACTION

How do you respond to unanticipated bad situations?

Immediate Action is a proactive eight-step process used to react to any bad situation that could cause a work stoppage, property damage, a security breach, or physical injury.

Let's drill down on the eight steps of the *Immediate Action* process.

Step 1. Assess the Situation.

Either be *on-the-scene* or in communication with someone on the ground. Assess the situation based on the facts.

Step 2. Notify Emergency Services and your boss.

If needed, call 911, and call your boss to tell him what you know.

Step 3. Consider your Options.

Look around. What's available for you to use? What should be done to stabilize the situation? What are your options? If time permits, collaborate with others.

Step 4. Select the Best Option.

Select the best option, and if time permits, achieve consensus with those around you.

Step 5. Create a Plan of Action.

Create a quick mental *Plan of Action*. What's the first step? What's the second, and so forth?

Step 6. Take Decisive Action.

Using what's available, *take-charge*, and give new instructions to others. Supervise their actions.

Step 7. Reassess the Situation.

What, if anything, has changed? Did the situation stabilize, or was the problem resolved? If Yes, move to Step 8. If NO, repeat this process.

Step 8. Call your boss.

Keep your boss informed. Explain what happened, what caused it, and what you recommend be done to ensure this never happens again. Sounds pretty easy, right? Well, let's see how it's done in the real world.

True Story

At 9 AM, two days before his company's annual Team Building Session, Bob, the Project Manager, conducted his final site inspection of the resort and was astonished by what he saw. He tried to pull into the resort, blocked by construction vehicles tearing up the parking lot. This was a disaster for Bob because he had 50 Senior Executives flying in from all over the country for this session. Fortunately, Bob knew how to take Immediate Action.

Step 1. Assess the Situation.

Bob didn't panic. He assessed the situation, took photos with his cell phone, spoke with the resort manager, and learned that a major water main had broken, which meant that the resort had no water. Bob also talked to the on-site construction manager and discovered that the water main could not be repaired for another week.

Step 2. Call Emergency Services and your boss.

At 9:30 AM: Since there was no need to call 911, Bob called his boss and appraised him of the situation.

Step 3. Consider your options.

At 10 AM, Bob called a meeting of all Key Players at company headquarters to collaborate to find the best solution. Bob asked one Key Player to find another venue that could accommodate 50 people.

By 11 AM, a new venue had been found, but it was 27 miles from the airport. One problem was solved, but it created another. How will all attendees get from the airport to the resort? Someone asked, can't they just catch a cab or just rent a car at the airport? For 50 people to catch a cab or rent a car would be way too expensive.

Step 4. Select the best option.

Then someone suggested that they rent a fleet of shuttle vehicles with drivers to transport all attendees from the airport to the resort and back. They all agreed that this was the best solution.

Step 5. Create a Plan of Action.

Together they created a Plan of Action to use shuttle vehicles to accomplish the objective.

Step 6. Take Decisive Action.

Bob issued new instructions to all Key Players and supervised their actions. He assigned one Key Player to contact all attendees to let them know what happened and look for company signs at the airport directing them to shuttle vehicles rather than taking a cab or renting a vehicle. Bob also asked a second Key Player to identify and contract a shuttle company to transport all attendees. Finally, he asked everyone to meet again at 5 PM to share the status of their new assignments.

Step 7. Reassess the Situation.

At 5 PM that afternoon, Bob met with all Key Players to ensure everything was ready to move forward with a fleet of shuttle vehicles.

Step 8. Report to your boss.

At 6 PM, Bob called his boss and informed him that the problem was resolved by selecting a new site and renting a fleet of shuttle vans to drive all attendees from the airport to the hotel and back. There was no reason to recommend what needed to be done to ensure this didn't happen again. The Team Building Session went on without any further problems and turned out to be a great success.

Bob looked defeat in the eye and refused to give up,

"Snatching Victory from the Jaws of Defeat."

And you can do the same!

This page is intentionally left blank.

G
ASSESS YOUR ACCOUNTABILITY

Do you know what to do when your boss finds something wrong with your work?

Accountability is the acceptance of responsibility for your actions and in-actions and the obligation to report, explain, and be answerable for any adverse consequences.

Accountability is often confused with responsibility. They're related but different. *Accountability* is normally not a problem - until something goes wrong.

For example, if something goes wrong within your area of responsibility, you'll get the chance to explain what happened to your boss, and maybe his boss. Sometimes, depending on the severity of the problem, your boss won't be happy with you and may treat you badly.

Most people don't understand that, yes, responsibility and *accountability* go together; they're part of the same iceberg.

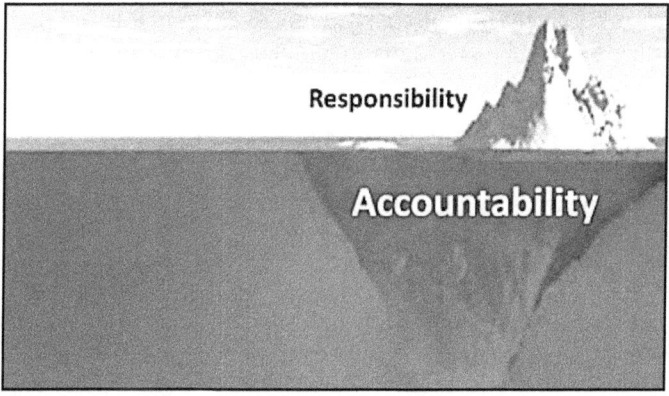

However, you can't see the *accountability* part of the iceberg because it lies hidden beneath the surface until something goes wrong.

What should you do when things go wrong?

When things go wrong for which you're responsible, your boss's job is to ask you for an explanation.

What your boss doesn't need is for you to blame others, make excuses, or hide the truth.

And yes, the mistake may have been made by one of your team members - not you. But your boss doesn't care. He just wants it fixed.

Here's what your boss expects you to do:

Step 1. Step up and accept the blame!

Step 2. Investigate - what happened and what caused it to happen?

Step 3. Report the facts and recommend how it should be fixed.

Step 4. Fix it and fix it for good!

Step 5. When fixed, report the fix to your boss.

Step 6. Make sure it never happens again.

Accountability is something every boss expects from you but won't tell you until it's too late. But, unfortunately, this quality isn't something you were born with. And the only time you get to demonstrate your accountability is when things go wrong.

This also includes the actions, in-actions, and adverse consequences of those members within your charge. You're accountable to your boss for everything that happens or fails to happen within your area of responsibility.

However, *accountability* can't exist unless you know all the things for which you're responsible. For example, you can't be held *accountable* for your company's finances if your duties and responsibilities are to service rental cars.

Establish the reputation of being a good problem solver as well as a good problem finder. Your job is to help your boss find and eliminate all the obstacles that could slow or stop the achievement of his goals.

Remember, mistakes, errors, and defects are not a problem if they're caught and fixed before getting in front of your boss or the customer.

Self-Test
Are you Accountable?

Here are the most important questions to answer to assess your *accountability*.

1. Do you do the right thing?

At an early age, I learned these simple lessons about accountability:

- If you lose, damage, or break something that doesn't belong to you, you need to fix it or buy it.

- If you borrow something, you need to return it in the same or better condition than you found it.

- If you back into and damage someone's car, and they're not around, you need to leave a note on their windshield with your name and phone number to help repair the damage.

- If you were mean or disrespectful to someone, you need to apologize.

2. Are you self-correcting?

A self-correcting person is someone capable of correcting himself without external help.

Part of being *accountable* is being *self-correcting*, especially when starting a new position, even if it's within the same company. Starting anything new is all about learning what you need to know as soon as possible. I'm always amazed by those who never take notes. Why do so few people take notes anymore (with your cell phone or Rocket Book)?

"A short pencil is a long memory." – Unknown.

When you have a question, write it down. Many times, the person with the correct answer won't be immediately available. If you find a term you don't understand, write it down. Later, find out what the term means. Keep a list of all your questions and terms you don't understand. This list will help later when you sponsor a new member into your team. *Self-correcting* people take notes (they don't trust their memory), write down their questions and the answers, and are not afraid to ask questions and proactively seek answers.

3. Do you live your life with no excuses?

People make excuses because it has worked for them in the past. It avoids accepting *accountability*. They're testing your limits to see how much they can get away with, and they fear the consequences of their actions or inactions.

What's the difference between a reason and an excuse?

Here's a simple rule:

Reasons are believable, understandable, and forgivable.

Excuses aren't.

Here are the commonly used excuses:

- **Denial:** Refusing to admit or acknowledge that their behavior is a problem. (Example: "I can stop swearing any time I want. My language isn't that bad.")

- **Isolation:** Removing themselves from the team area to maintain their behavior. (Example: "If I had my own office, this wouldn't be a problem.")

- **Rationalization:** Giving reasons to explain their behavior. (Example: "I screamed at him because he doesn't like me.")

- **Blaming (or Transferal):** Transferring *accountability* for their behavior to others. (Example: "I wouldn't be late all the time if my teammates treated me right.")

- **Projection:** Rejecting their feelings by ascribing them to another (Example: "Why is that stupid idiot so hostile?")

- **Minimizing or Trivialize:** Refusing to admit the effect of their behavior. (Example: "I only told one bad joke. It's not a big deal.")

They close their eyes to the destructive consequences of their unacceptable behavior, or they explain their actions in a way that saves them from having to feel. Either way, it's wrong and must be dealt with immediately.

4. Do you do your best work every day?

Here's a great story about doing your best work.

*It's rumored that when Dr. **Henry Kissinger** was Secretary of State in the administrations of **Presidents Nixon and Ford**, he asked for a security assessment to be made of a foreign country.*

The first day, when a subordinate delivered the report, Secretary Kissinger asked, "Is this your best work?"

The subordinate thought for a second and walked out of the office. The second day, the subordinate returned with the report, and Kissinger asked the same question. The subordinate again thought for a moment and walked back out of the office.

On the third day, the subordinate returned, and Kissinger asked for the third time, "Is this your best work?" This time the subordinate said, "Yes." Kissinger then responded, "Good, now I'll read it."

I share this story to highlight that there are no shortcuts to success. Your success will always be linked to *"doing your best work."* Do you do your best work every day? Would your boss agree?

5. Are you proactive?

Another thing that contributes to your effectiveness and success at work is your ability to be proactive.

A proactive person identifies and prevents potential problems by causing things to happen rather than reacting to them after they happen.

Proactive people:

- Identify potential pre-problems (Chapter 6) before they become a problem and problems before they become a crisis.

- Anticipate their boss's and customer's needs and expectations,

- Use Preventive Actions (Chapter 6) to identify and resolve all Pre-Problems.

- Take-charge (Chapter 11) and produce order in the midst of chaos.

- Use collaborative problem-solving to build consensus (Chapter 16) and resolve Unresolved Issues (Chapter 9)

- Take Immediate Action (Appendix F) and don't wait to be told what to do.

- Anticipate Unintended Consequences and 2d and 3d Order Effects (Chapter 10)

- Manage risk (Chapters 17-19) and make things happen the right way the first time.

6. Do you make recommendations to your boss to make things better?

Your job is to help your boss achieve his goals. What do you do when you find a problem or an improvement that could make things better? Do you create a *Decision Paper* or a *Business Case* (Appendix E) to make it happen?

I've often written Decision Papers through my boss to his boss because my boss didn't have the funding to make it happen. As shown below, the Decision Paper was addressed "To," my boss's boss, "Thru," my boss.

To: My boss's boss.

Thru: My boss.

From: Me

My boss would then initial and write "Approved" next to the "Thru" line above and send it to his boss for final approval. This process helped my boss move the work forward.

If you cannot answer these questions with a strong YES, you need to reassess your *accountability*. Effective people take this assessment annually and fix what needs to be fixed.

ACKNOWLEDGMENTS

"Many people will walk in and out of your life, but only
true friends will leave footprints in your heart."
- Eleanor Roosevelt

I'd like to recognize those with whom I've had the pleasure of serving, whose effectiveness and character I vividly recall, many of whom are not here today to tell their story.

For my military career, I thank Betty McIntee, Edward J. Murphy (my Dad), Dale R. Nelson, Geoffrey "Jeff" Prosch, Craig "Randy" Rutler, Dave Wagner, John Andrews, John "The Bear" Warren, John "Jack" Costello, Dan Labin, and Ron Nicholl for their example of effectiveness.

For my coaching career, I thank Tony Robbins, Bernard Haldane, Jack Bissell, Len Drew, Wayne McCullum, Bob Schrier, John Hurtig, and Bob Gerberg for their mentoring and coaching.

Special thanks to my long-time mentor and friend, Joyce Kuntz, who encouraged me to write this book. After leaving the US Military, Joyce was my first and best boss when I joined her consulting firm in Seattle years ago. Unfortunately, Joyce is gone now, but her legacy lives on in this book.

"I must be able to say with sincerity that to see things differently is a
strength, not a weakness, in my relationship with others."
- Joyce Kuntz

I thank Joyce's husband, Ed Kuntz, who turned out to be the man who brought me to Seattle from Kansas City to start my incredible second career as an Executive Coach.

And finally, I thank my soulmate and wife, ***Diana***, for her love, encouragement, and understanding throughout this process.

When I count my blessings, I always count her twice.

ABOUT THE AUTHOR

"I expect to pass through this world but once; any good thing therefore that I can do, or any kindness that I can show to any fellow creature, let me do it now; let me not defer or neglect it, for I shall not pass this way again."
- Stephan Grelle

Ed Murphy considers himself lucky. From age 7, he knew what he wanted to be when he grew up. He wanted to be a Soldier. So, four days after graduating from High School, he joined the US Army and found himself in Basic Training and Advanced Infantry Training at Fort Dix, New Jersey.

A year later, Ed became a Cadet at the United States Military Academy at West Point. In 1970, he graduated as a 2d Lieutenant headed to Airborne and Ranger School, then off to Viet Nam for a year.

In 1978, Ed returned to West Point to teach Military Science and earned an MS from LIU in night school. During his tenure as a Battalion Commander in West Germany, his greatest achievement was helping 1400 soldiers begin a college education. He wanted to give his soldiers something of real value - something that no one could ever take away. After 23 years as a US Army Officer, he retired in 1993.

For his second career, with help from *Tony Robbins*, he became an Executive Coach. Then, for the next 21 years, he worked for four career development and outplacement companies in America, from Seattle, San Diego, Kansas City, and Phoenix.

In 2012, Ed retired a second time and decided to document everything he learned from those he most admired during his 50+ years in the US Military as an Army Officer and Corporate America as an Executive Coach.

In 2014, he began writing books for Amazon and Kindle dedicated to providing the best-in-class wisdom, knowledge, and advice to help others maximize their true career potential by becoming more effective and successful at work and in life.

Today, Ed considers himself blessed to get to live in Phoenix, AZ. He enjoys writing, eating sushi, genealogy, and watching movies with family, friends, and his best friend and wife, *Diana.*

CONCLUSION

Congratulations!

And thank you for joining us on this *Journey of Discovery*.

As promised, you now have a *Planning Guide* to add to your professional library - the one I never had.

Every effective boss needs effective followers who can consistently produce excellent results and add value to those who helped produce those results.

You now have the most actionable *Planning Skills* you were never taught in school or college to support you throughout your career.

Now it's your turn to apply and share this new knowledge to add greater value to your boss and all those with whom you serve.

These are the essential *Best Practices* I've learned over the past 50 years to help you become far more effective and successful than you were yesterday.

As always, I wish you great success.

Never STOP Learning!

Ed

Founder of *The Effectiveness Institute*

email: ed.murphy77@gmail.com

PS: Also, if you feel this information could help someone else, please let them know. If it turns out to make a difference in their life, they'll be forever grateful to you, as will I.

Stop wishing you were better and do something about it today.

www.ingramcontent.com/pod-product-compliance
Lightning Source LLC
Chambersburg PA
CBHW051915170526
45168CB00001B/394